Careers in Sales

2006 Edition

WetFeet Insider Guide

WetFeet, Inc.

The Folger Building
101 Howard Street
Suite 300
San Francisco, CA 94105

Phone: (415) 284-7900 or 1-800-926-4JOB
Fax: (415) 284-7910
Website: www.WetFeet.com

Careers in Sales

2006 Edition
ISBN: 1-58207-541-7

Table of Contents

The Workplace. 95

Getting Hired 115

For Your Reference. 127

Sales at a Glance

Opportunity Overview

- Sales plays an essential part in any business, large or small, public or private. Therefore, the need for highly qualified salespeople exists within every industry from real estate to technology.

- Sales opportunities aren't limited by geographic region. Sales reps can work as field agents across the country, living great distances from corporate headquarters. Wherever there are consumers, there's a need for salespeople.

- Compensation opportunities are vast and varied, offering the possibility of incomes reaching $100,000 or more for those with the right skill set and motivation level. Additional earnings come in the form of commissions and bonuses.

- Most companies offer some type of in-house training program designed to prepare sales representatives for the field. The larger the company, the more training offered.

- The field of sales is a competitive arena with a high turnover rate. It requires strong communication and organizational skills, self-motivation, and the ability to work well under pressure.

Major Pluses about Sales Careers

- Successful salespeople can be very well-compensated for their work. Most careers in sales are based on a commission structure offering the possibility of hefty payouts for large sales.

- A wide range of sales career opportunities exists within all industries—from field reps working alone to sales managers responsible for leading diverse teams.

- Nontraditional working environments offer flexible hours, the opportunity to telecommute from a home office, and the prospect of travel.

- Many companies offer a wide range of benefits and perks—from comprehensive health packages to educational reimbursement plans.

Major Minuses about Sales Careers

- The hours are long and may include late-night and weekend work.

- Product information can be extensive and complex, requiring rigorous job training and an ability to thoroughly understand complicated material.

- When the economy is weak and companies are forced to downsize, even greater pressure is placed on sales professionals to produce.

- Sales quotas can be challenging to meet due to a sophisticated and ever more complex marketplace. This pressure can lead to anxiety over job stability.

- Competition among sales reps across an industry is fierce, quickly weeding out those lacking the aptitude and skill set to deal with the demanding environment.

Recruiting Overview

- New college graduates with a minor or major in a field that complements the industry they wish to join are most marketable. Sales experience is also important.

- Companies recruit recent graduates and MBAs at campus career fairs, trade shows, and conferences throughout the year.

- Job postings can be found in newspapers, on Internet job boards, and on individual company websites.

- Large companies often hire individual and Web-based recruiters to find the best qualified candidates to fill sales positions.

- Often, companies will extend job offers to highly successful sales representatives working for competitors.

- You can obtain interviews by building strong networks within an industry of interest and directly contacting those in charge of sales.

- Internship experiences and personal networking are also key to breaking into a desired industry.

The Role

Opportunity Overview

A sales career can take on many faces whether it's that of a real estate agent selling beachfront property or a consumer rep landing a major account with a large retailer. From your favorite cereal on the grocery store shelf to the antibiotic prescribed by your doctor, sales has had a hand. And no matter what the industry, the role of the salesperson to his or her employer is one of great importance—a key contributor to the bottom line. Without a highly skilled and motivated sales staff, businesses of all kinds would be writing their obituaries. Sales is a very competitive field that offers good communicators, self-starters, and product experts the opportunity to earn high incomes. But the pressure to produce, especially in a field where compensation is performance-based, can mean quick turnover and job instability. It's a world of big profit and small margin for failure.

When we talk about sales, we're referring to those people who provide customers or companies with a specific good or service, fulfilling a mutual need on both parts of the relationship. You've probably already taken part in the process, toting those ever-popular Girl Scout Thin Mints or magazine subscriptions from door to door. But even if you've never experienced the thrill of the sale, you've definitely been a part of the audience. Just one glimpse of a Super Bowl commercial and you realize how many big bucks are spent each day pushing new products and services. The result: endless opportunities across all industries.

In fact, the field of sales is so vast that the U.S. Department of Labor has listed more than 20 occupational groups within the classification alone, ranging from counter clerks to financial service providers. What vary are the products or services on offer and the audience the seller hopes to reach. Salespeople have also taken on a new persona as problem solvers and consultants, making the image of the unannounced man in a tweed jacket with a suitcase of encyclopedias a thing of the past.

Working in sales can take on so many definitions that those seeking a career in this field should first understand the key components involved in selling to weigh its appeal. As a sales representative in any industry, your main objective is to sell your product or service to as many clients as possible to earn a profit for your company. This may take the form of traditional cold-calling—the act of initiating contact with potential customers—to large presentations in front of entire purchasing teams. But no matter the format, closing deals is your ultimate goal. Being a part of the industry also requires interacting well in face-to-face situations. Whether you're a clerk at a local retail store or a pharmaceutical representative making office visits to doctors, communication skills and congeniality are a must for a successful sales career. You must be a self-starter who is not averse to putting in the time needed to build a strong client base. And talk about high stress. There's the pressure of limited time, savvy customers, and high sales expectations. And although training is provided, sales representatives are expected to drive their own sales process. This involves maintaining a constant pipeline of opportunities, as well as extensive travel, endless follow-up calls, and late nights spent preparing presentations.

Given the far reach of the field of sales, into just about any industry you can imagine, and the varied nature of the sales function from industry to industry, it would be impossible to describe the work of sales in any depth without narrowing our focus. To that end, this guide considers the field of sales as it plays out in six high-end industries that rely heavily on, and offer the majority of opportunities, for sales professionals: pharmaceuticals and biotech, technology, financial services, insurance, manufacturing, and real estate. Despite this book's focus on the role of sales in these six industries, there are a host of opportunities for sales professionals in other industries. Due to the diverse and numerous sales roles within each of these industries, candidates are advised to keep an open mind when focusing on their individual career paths. Not only will sales roles vary from company to company, so will their labels, taking on titles such as account executive or sales representative.

In addition to offering opportunities in nearly any industry, the field of sales as a whole employs workers from a vast array of ages and backgrounds, from recent college graduates to seasoned professionals with decades of experience, from men to women and ethnic minorities. It's a dynamic, fast-paced world with endless possibilities for growth and financial success. And for those with the right skills, it's a fertile playground of opportunities.

The Playing Field

Whenever interest rates begin to rise and consumer spending drops, pressure is immediately placed on sales divisions to come up with a solution. As research and development teams compete to improve products, sales divisions must also adapt their selling process to those changing products. Products and services already in the market are being mimicked or advanced daily. With so much competition, companies must constantly find new ways to redefine the value of their products or services. Furthermore, to remain viable, companies must effectively recruit, train, and retain top-performing salespeople. For the sales rep out in the field, this means that the old technique of presenting the bells and whistles of a product no longer works. And who has time for a round of golf to secure a deal? The audience has become more sophisticated; it is turned off by persuasion. As one insider in the sales consulting field says, "Sales reps today need to be problem solvers instead of product pushers."

With the increased demands placed on sales teams comes a shift in many corporate cultures and recruiting processes. To impress potential employers, candidates must do their research, stepping into interviews with a thorough knowledge of the company's product or service. Companies often recruit new talent from job fairs, trade shows, and conferences; they look for people from all walks of life with strong communication skills, selling experience, and enthusiasm.

While the job outlook for most sales positions across the board remains strong, sales opportunities vary by industry. Overall, sales opportunities are projected to grow as fast as the average growth rate, according to the U.S. Bureau of Labor Statistics (BLS), which means a 10 to 20 percent increase through 2012. High-growth industries such as financial services are seeing a greater demand for sales roles than the more mature, slower-growth industries such as manufacturing and real estate. Technology, especially the Internet, has changed the playing field. In the past, customers relied on sales representatives to educate them about the latest trends, product details, and price comparisons. But today, with the right search engine, a few free minutes, and a cable connection, access to information previously limited to those working in the field is available to everyone. This new self-service trend has made the car salesman and travel agent almost obsolete. To compete, salespeople must adapt and become consultants able to connect the value of a product or service to a client's specific needs.

Changing of the Guard

When you think of sales, you may think about a recent home-cooked meal or TV show cliffhanger that was interrupted by a phone call with some all-too-familiar pitch: "Hey, if I could make you $10,000, would you be interested?"

For those with a wary eye toward sales, a dramatic new wave in selling practices is overtaking the industry. Sales veterans may still hold fast to traditional methods, but those breaking into the business need to heed the latest trends to be competitive. The overall emphasis in the field today is on the psychology of sales. Companies are not only looking to better understand buyers, they also want to understand the mindset of successful sellers. This shift in focus is required by a more informed audience and the fierce competition that now characterizes so many industries.

TRADITIONAL SCHOOL OF THOUGHT

The prevailing stereotype of the fast-talking salesman who doesn't let his customer get a word in edgewise is a result of traditional sales techniques once believed to be effective in getting customers to buy a given product or service. This kind of salesman is seen as ruthless, manipulative, and money-driven. It's no wonder many people become uneasy when they think about dealing with salespeople in any industry, whether to buy a phone or to extend health coverage. The old school of thought is based on coercing the customer through a features-and-benefits, "act now to get a great deal" selling process that includes trumpeting all of the bells and whistles of a product or service to justify the price. The belief is that, if the sales rep does a good enough job of presenting the product or service in a pleasing manner, a sale will be made.

Many who still depend on older selling methods also use the "get to the yes" approach, which involves asking a customer several leading questions—often, "Would you like a product that can solve your problem?" and "Would you like to save money?"—in the hope that the yeses will keep flowing when they finally get to the question, "Would you like to buy my product?" This sales methodology also bases its success in the law of numbers, meaning that the more calls a sales rep makes, the more sales he or she will produce over time.

Sales reps who use these traditional approaches are often perceived as dynamic individuals able to build strong relationships with their charismatic style. These practices are still prevalent as they do still work and are more cost-effective for companies looking to avoid new training expenses. But performing a song-and-dance routine every time you approach a new prospect is not only exhausting, it's also proving less-effective, which is why many salespeople are turning to a new school of thought.

NEW SCHOOL OF THOUGHT

These days, customers are not so easily manipulated and have less time to spend being courted by sales reps hoping to close a deal. So sales reps have had to become more knowledgeable, savvy communicators who can instantly define a customer's pain and offer a customized solution. (Nearly every product and service today is termed a "solution" in today's sales pitch. Why?) Extensive research into the psychology of the buyer and seller is influencing the sales methodology in many companies. When planning strategy around bringing products and services to market, many companies are now seeking to answer two questions: "What is the emotional motivation behind buying decisions?" and "What is the thought process of successful sales reps?"

This seismic shift has led many companies to adopt a more consultative style of selling, as opposed to one that merely presents the features of the products and services being offered. Sales reps are now encouraged to become problem-solvers able to tailor their products and services to meet the needs of the client. Often sales reps will refer to themselves as consultants looking to form relationships with their customers in order to work together to create the perfect deal. Complex strategic sales processes are generated by sales teams well before contact with a potential client is made. A sales rep must know a company's decision makers, buying habits, financial budget, and history. No longer can a sales rep wing a presentation and expect to close a deal. As a result of these changes, ongoing training is a significant part of most sales reps' jobs. With the shift toward more consultative, relational, and strategy-based selling, those not willing to change are finding themselves left behind.

OLD SCHOOL TO NEW SCHOOL

Training styles like the products and services they help sell are constantly changing to meet the competitive demands of the market. There's a definite old school style versus new school approach, and although companies are starting to move toward new advances in the field, some old, reliable practices are still in place.

Old School	New School
Training	
Not much formal training on all industry levels. Most training is apprentice style, in which sales reps learn the ropes from a seasoned rep. Formal training is limited to a company manual covering product specifications along with company policies and procedures.	Large companies: Extensive training throughout the year usually handled by a training department within the company. Additional resources, such as outside consultants and coaches, used by teams and individuals to improve performance. Small companies: Less formal training. Most training is conducted in-house through mentoring programs between senior staff and new hires. Small companies may also turn to outside sources, such as consultants and workshops, for further training.
Approach	
Features and benefits selling: Reps show off the bells and whistles of the product to justify price to customers.	Consultative, strategic account managing, and relational selling: Reps act as consultants looking to build personal relationships with their customers in a strategic approach to the selling process.
Audience	
Uninformed audience relies on sales reps to provide information on products and services.	Sophisticated, knowledgeable audience that typically has already done research before sales presentations.
Strategy	
Law of numbers: The more calls you make, the more business you will eventually gain.	Understanding the psychology of the seller and buyer: What are the emotions behind purchasing decisions? How do successful sales reps think?
Rep	
Fast-talking sales reps who use manipulation to persuade customers into making a purchase.	Problem-solvers who listen to their clients' needs and are able to customize their product or service to meet those needs.
Closing	
Days of wining and dining, where 18 holes of golf and a swanky meal are all it takes to close a deal.	Time is precious, so reps must use what little time they get in front of their customers to present the value of their product or service.

Where to Start?

For those candidates with solid resumes and strong interview skills, a day spent at a college campus job fair will result in several job offers from various companies. The companies making these offers will vary from small to large, private to public. And although being wanted by many companies may come as a relief for a college grad who's been living on mac and cheese for the last 4 years, narrowing down the job field raises many questions. When choosing among offers, many candidates wonder whether working for a large company is more advantageous than working for a small firm. Yes, there's the prestige assigned with the former, but what about the exciting growth that a small company can offer?

Before considering the size of a company, it's best to also note whether the company is privately held or publicly traded. And although you will find exceptions to many commonly held beliefs about the cultures associated with both types, certain traits often set the two apart.

PRIVATE VS PUBLIC

Privately held companies are generally smaller in size than those that are publicly traded. Typically, the smaller the company, the fewer rules and procedures there are in place. Job titles aren't as defined, allowing for more crossover between divisions and more input from employees. There's usually more of a family feel to the overall culture of a privately held company; employees are encouraged to take an active part in the company's overall growth, fostering a sense of loyalty and excitement. The ease with which some privately held companies operate is mainly due to the fact that they don't have to report on their performance to shareholders. Without the added pressure of investors watching over their shoulders, private companies have much more room for entrepreneurial savvy. The culture is often more open to individuality. Companies may even base decisions on principles such as environment or community impact.

When a company grows and takes on shareholders, it tends to become more standardized in its procedures. There are just too many voices at all levels of the corporation to customize operations to meet the individual needs of employees. Measures of revenue, profit, and return on investment are heavily weighted and scrutinized by investors, placing more pressure on those in the field to produce.

Of course, public companies also offer some benefits that their privately held counterparts can't: Public companies can offer valuable stock options to their employees. With more money at their disposal, they are also more stable than privately held firms. Publicly traded companies also generally offer a wider range of products for their reps to sell and have the means to constantly research the market and make changes necessary to stay competitive. Conversely, their size and dependence on shareholders can also make publicly traded companies slower to act and more risk-averse than some private companies.

BIG VS SMALL

Many of the same characteristics that hold true for private firms can be applied to smaller companies with fewer than 500 employees. Known for more laid-back, innovative cultures and more close-knit work environments, smaller companies have received plenty of kudos in the last few years when it comes to job opportunities. During the dot-com era, one of the hottest job trends was to land a position with a start-up company in its early years, in hopes of cashing in once it went public. (Most dot-com start-ups offered early employees stock options.) With the slow pace of initial public offerings today, the opportunities for jackpot job opportunities like those have diminished. However, small companies still offer many rewards.

Smaller companies are often younger or family-owned operations that fill a niche in the market. They tend to be headquartered in rural or suburban areas where costs can be minimized. This may also means less money for base salaries and benefit packages than those offered at larger companies. Smaller companies often operate with fewer rules and regulations. Training programs are often not as extensive, though this doesn't apply in all cases, as a smaller environment can sometimes mean that junior personnel receive more one-on-one attention from senior employees. Employees in small companies are often assigned more responsibilities, and their performance is more visible to management. Smaller companies also often afford their employees more opportunities to directly influence decision-making instead of simply taking direction from senior management. And although there isn't as much opportunity for career advancement as there is in a larger company, there may be more chances for future ownership in the organization. Overall, there's a general buzz that comes from feeling like an integral part of a company's growth, where every employee's actions contribute to the company's overall success. On the other hand, in struggling smaller businesses, the pressure on employees can be intense.

When talking about larger companies, we are referring to those Fortune 500 firms typically headquartered close to or in metropolitan areas. They are familiar names and often supply the household products that clutter our shelves but that we can't live without. One of the most distinguishing features is their public rating score within the stock market. For new employees this can mean extra earnings in the form of stock options and profit sharing along with the prestige that comes with saying that you work at one of the leading companies in your industry. Large companies have extensive training programs for their sales forces, offering bringing them together for training several times a year. Making sure their reps are updated on the latest product trends takes top priority. There are also clear career tracks for those motivated to move up the ranks of a corporate structure. With larger resource pools, these companies also typically offer larger salary and bonus opportunities. And because they also tend to work with other large companies, sales deals involve higher budgets that can translate into substantial commissions for reps. The role of an employee within a large company is also more defined; this can sometimes feel limiting. Not as much attention is placed on the individual needs of employees within a large organization, and the overall culture is much more conservative, with strict policies and procedures for all company operations. Large firms often make it their goal to recruit the best and in turn place high expectations on their employees.

Taking the Temp

Much like a game of hot and cold, the closer a company is to dominating a market with its product or service, the hotter it becomes. But to match and even beat the competition, companies must constantly reinvent their products and services. For some industries, failure to find a way to stay current with the needs of the market has meant severe downsizing and even closures, ultimately resulting in stunted job growth for incoming sales reps. The increasing use of global technology has also had a large impact on the field of sales, at times enabling companies to better serve clients while also giving clients the tools they need to serve themselves.

FEELING THE FREEZE

Although the real estate market has witnessed some of its largest appreciation levels in years, many economists predict that with the inevitable rise of interest rates it is heading for slower times. The industry is already saturated with experienced agents and brokers, making it more difficult for those breaking into the business. One of the main reasons for this decline is the influence of information technology. In an effort to avoid paying commission fees, many buyers are now conducting their own searches on the Internet when looking for a home. With the percentage of sale purchases still rising, opportunities exist for those wishing to work in the field. But the days of commission feasting may soon be over, and if so, those entering the field will find long hours and constant lead generating have taken its place.

Another sales position expected to grow more slowly than the average according to the BLS is that of the insurance agent. Although a large number of existing agents are expected to retire in the upcoming years and overall insurance demands will rise with a growing population, the need for new agents is dwindling. To cut costs, many insurance carriers are no longer hiring agents to sell their products but are turning to other outlets such as direct marketing and independent contractors. The increasing reach of the financial services industry into products and services previously unassociated with that industry has also taken a bite out of the insurance agent's pie. Many people now turn to financial services agents for insurance polices, along with other products related to long-term financial planning.

For salespeople in every industry, a constant battle rages against being viewed by potential customers as just one of many sales reps with similar products knocking on the door. When this happens, sales reps find themselves standing in line at a potential client's door, waiting to take their turn in a long row of presentations, as if auditioning for a part. The uniqueness and personal connection are often lost as sales reps from competing companies attempt to outshine their competition. And with the buyer in the driver's seat, negotiations can become intense. To combat this problem, companies are forever trying to reinvent themselves, hoping to strike gold with a one-of-a-kind product or service that will sweep the market.

WHAT'S HOT

According to several surveys by various recruiting companies, the financial sales rep position is one of the hottest careers of the next 10 years. The BLS also reports that sales careers in securities, commodities, and financial services will grow about as fast as the average through the year 2012. This translates into a 10 to 20 percent increase in job opportunities. Why is this industry growing so fast? One of the effects of the failing economy over the last 5 years is a shift in the public's investing attitudes. No longer are people expecting short-term returns on their investments. Rather they are turning to long-term financial planning as a safer alternative. With so many people looking for help managing their personal wealth, financial sales rep will undoubtedly become a sought-after profession.

Another factor influencing sales job growth, one not tied to a specific industry, is the drive for companies to find their own niche within a specific marketplace. When a company develops a product or service that successfully satisfies a need of a designated audience, an avalanche of profits soon follow. This is why companies spend millions in research and marketing to find that need that has not yet been satisfied. Working as a sales rep within a trendy niche market where demand for your product is high is the holy grail of sales: It's what every sales professional hopes for. In other words, finding a niche trend in your industry is one key to a successful career.

For example, two hot trends in the technology industry include wireless hardware and security software products. The craze to go wireless is everywhere—from the Internet connection on our traveling laptops to the personal use of cell phones in the air. Wireless hardware sales include a wide range of products from routers to personal digital assistants (PDAs). On the software side of technology, the threat of terrorism and reality of identity theft are driving new software product research. Demand for software that can aid in early detection of terrorist activity is on the rise. And as more people each day turn to online systems for their banking and shopping needs, the need for online security is ever more important. And this demand is further fueled by the growing concern around the rash of database break-ins that have exposed the personal information of thousands of people.

Pharmaceutical companies are also looking to pull in the reigns on their product focus in response to increasing lawsuits over the hidden side effects of many new drugs hitting the market. Instead of developing mega-drugs, many companies now hope to corner niche therapeutic areas. Drugs that target very specific illnesses are more profitable, for a few key reasons. They carry less liability as they tend to have fewer side effects. They can be tested on smaller groups before going to market, and once shown to be effective they can monopolize a market. Pharmaceutical reps selling niche drugs also find that doctors are more eager to see them, which sure beats feeling like a 90-second sound byte in between coffee sips.

The Industries

Pharmaceuticals and Biotechnology

Technology

Financial Services

Insurance

Manufacturing

Real Estate

Pharmaceuticals and Biotechnology

Most of us are familiar with the frustration of showing up for a doctor's appointment on time, only to be forced to wait 20 or 30 minutes or more before seeing the doctor. Imagine dropping in as a sales rep for a drug company and trying to get a few moments of that same doctor's time. It's not an easy task. In fact, an industry manager in the spring 2005 issue of *Microsoft Executive Circle* reported that often pharmaceutical sales reps get about a 90-second window in which to present their wares. As one insider says, "Making contact with a doctor can be difficult, especially for first-time calls. Doctors who work in clinics or small practices with heavy workloads just don't have the time to spend listening to reps. This is why it's so important to know your product in and out and be able to present it in a quick, efficient manner."

With this kind of pressure, you might wonder why so many people are eager to land a job in pharmaceutical sales. Careers in pharmaceutical sales are very attractive because the pharmaceutical industry has been experiencing stable growth in general. There's a constant need for new and improved drugs in the marketplace—this means that a pharmaceutical rep, if successful, has a better chance at a long-term career with the same company in this industry than in a more competitive industry, such as technology or financial services, where sales reps are often under more pressure to meet larger quotas. In addition, working within the health industry usually offers great health benefits as well as the opportunity to develop personal relationships with doctors, who then keep them abreast of the latest trends in the medical community. To top that off, some pharmaceutical companies offer perks such as bonuses in the form of monetary incentives or vacation packages at luxury resorts.

INDUSTRY OVERVIEW

Pharmaceutical companies produce and market drugs, from familiar over-the-counter compounds such as aspirin to exotic prescriptions that inhibit, activate, or otherwise affect individual molecules involved in specific medical conditions.

The pharmaceutical drug discovery and development industry has grown to become one of the most profitable in the world, with drug companies posting billions of dollars in profits each year. During the last 30 years, the industry has blossomed, with billions of dollars put back into research in biochemistry, molecular biology, cell biology, immunology, genetics, and information technology—and billions of dollars in profits earned by drug companies. Indeed, in 2004, the pharmaceutical industry sold $550 billion in pharmaceutical products worldwide, according to a survey by *Pharmaceutical Magazine*.

In recent years, the pharmaceutical industry has performed exceedingly well relative to other industries. Though there's plenty of public controversy (e.g., around the moral and ethical questions surrounding genomics and the pricing and patent practices of Big Pharma— insider shorthand for the handful of multinational giants that dominate the industry), demand for drugs is growing, fueled by an aging population and blossoming international markets. Regardless of whether you choose to work for Big Pharma or a small biotech, don't get too attached to the status quo. These days, the business environment can change overnight. You only need to look at recent biotech stock volatility for ample evidence of such change. And as one insider says, "Even in Big Pharma, if there's a merger or a spinoff, you can easily find yourself without a job."

> **Doctors who work in clinics or small practices with heavy workloads just don't have the time to spend listening to reps. This is why it's so important to know your product in and out and be able to present it in a quick, efficient manner.**

INDUSTRY SECTORS

Pharmaceuticals

The majority of Big Pharma companies are headquartered in the United States, but several are based in Western Europe—in Switzerland, Germany, and France. Those headquartered in the United States are all located east of the Mississippi, with the greatest concentration in New Jersey. Big Pharma companies come in two styles: diversified and nondiversified. Diversified companies—which include Johnson & Johnson, Abbott Laboratories, and Wyeth, maintain other health care–related businesses, such as consumer health product divisions and medical device companies, while those that are nondiversified—such as Eli Lilly and Merck—focus solely on the development and sale of drugs. Over the past few years, some diversified companies opted to divest their nonpharmaceutical concerns in favor of the leaner and more profitable drug business. Bristol-Myers Squibb, for instance, sold Clairol, the number-one hair-products company in the United States, to Procter & Gamble in 2001.

Biotechnology

Despite the success of such biotech giants as Amgen and Genentech, a large majority of biotech shops are still small enough for everyone to know everyone else's name. But a growing number is joining the elite group of biotech firms that have FDA-approved drugs on the market; between 2000 and 2004, the FDA approved some 170 new drugs and vaccines and new indications for existing products. Once a biotech company has reached the stage at which it has a product coming to market, its jobs expand from the primarily science-focused to include marketing, manufacturing, engineering, and, of particular interest to you, dear reader, sales.

Key Pharmaceutical Companies

Company	2004 Revenue ($M)	1-Year Change (%)	Employees
Pfizer	52,516	16.2	115,000
Johnson & Johnson	47,348	13.1	109,900
Bayer AG	40,310	12.2	113,825
GlaxoSmithKline	39,032	2.1	100,019
Novartis AG	28,247	13.6	81,392
Roche Holding	27,630	9.9	64,703
Merck & Co.	22,939	2.0	63,000
AstraZeneca	21,426	13.7	64,000
Sanofi-Aventis	20,377	101.4	96,439
Abbott Laboratories	19,680	0	60,600

Sources: Hoover's; WetFeet analysis.

Key Biotech Companies

Company	2004 Revenue ($M)	1-Year Change (%)	Employees
Amgen	10,550	26.3	14,400
Genentech	3,980	42.2	7,646
Biogen Idec	2,212	225.6	4,266
Genzyme Corp.	2,201	28.4	7,100
Serono S.A.	2,178	17.2	4,740
Applera Corp.	1,825	2.7	5,360
Chiron Corp.	1,723	−2.4	5,400
Gilead Sciences	1,325	52.6	1,654
MedImmune	1,141	8.2	1,976
Covance	1,056	8.4	6,700

Sources: Hoover's; WetFeet analysis.

INDUSTRY TRENDS

The Cost of Research

Insiders say the biggest issue the industry currently faces is around the question of who will pay for the rising cost of drug development. Prescription drug prices are rising annually, while insurers have become increasingly stringent about which medications they offer reimbursement for. Promising new breakthrough drugs can cost thousands or even tens of thousands of dollars per treatment. Providing price relief for seniors has been an issue for several years now. Many favor price controls to prevent costs from skyrocketing, a move opposed by the pharmaceutical industry, which in turn has the support of the current administration.

Drug companies contend that they must charge a premium for patented drugs and protect their patents because this is the only way they can generate sufficient revenue to pay for the continued research that leads to the discovery of new medicines. (Critics respond by pointing out that the industry spends much more on marketing than on research and development.)

O Canada

Many patients have been responding to high drug prices by buying drugs at lower cost from other countries. Canada is the country in the spotlight these days, as it ships a high volume of pharmaceuticals to patients in America. But importing prescription drugs is illegal in the United States—and, according to the FDA, unsafe. The pharma companies hate this trend, of course, because their profits will suffer if people can buy drugs at cheaper prices than the drug companies charge in the United States.

In the United States, legislators are pushing to legalize the import of prescription drugs over the Internet from Canada. A number of lobbying organizations in the United States, meanwhile, have criticized Big Pharma on behalf of their citizens, who, they say, should be able to buy drugs at the lower prices they can get by importing them.

Trouble in Paradise?

There's a dearth of new drugs coming to market these days. In 2004, the FDA approved just 21 new drugs, compared to 53 in 1996. Why? Industry observers point to a number of possible reasons. For one thing, the genomics revolution has not been as successful as biotech companies and their investors had hoped it would be—at least, not so far. For another, a decade or so ago, pharmaceutical companies changed the way they discovered new drugs. Instead of letting lab scientists do what they'd always done—which included exploring their hunches—they took to creating thousands of chemical combinations and testing their drug potential using robots. This was supposed to be a faster, cheaper way of finding new drugs. Instead, it's turned out to be an ineffective means of drug discovery.

Meanwhile, with key patents expiring or set to expire in the near future, biotech and pharmaceutical companies are facing increasing pressure to come up with new marketable products, since investors demand that companies' growth charts point ever upward. The result is that pharmaceutical and biotech firms alike are focusing on squeezing more and more revenue out of fewer and fewer drugs.

SALES ROLES

Pharmaceutical companies employ a variety of people in different sales positions. Field sales reps call on doctors, hospitals, and HMOs. District managers usually manage ten to 14 field reps, hiring, training, and supervising them; area managers oversee the district managers. The act of selling to doctors is widely known as *detailing*, particularly if the salesperson uses company-produced visual aids.

The field is also very competitive, with more than one rep for a specific drug or product soliciting the same business. To stand apart from the crowd, reps are expected to become experts in their fields, able to handle any battery of questions fired at them by a prospective client physician or other health-care professional.

Pharmaceutical Sales Representative

Pharmaceutical sales reps work with physicians, hospitals, health maintenance organizations (HMOs), and countless other medical institutions to keep health-care professionals abreast of—and, if possible, partial toward—their company's line of products.

Depending on the assigned territory, some of these jobs require local and regional travel; others do not. Reps service territories that are typically defined by both specialty and geography (e.g., all primary care doctors in Omaha, or all cardiologists in New Hampshire) and operate under a prescribed call cycle that determines how often they visit each doctor in their territory. Call cycles range from 2 weeks to 4 months for most drugs, but they can sometimes be as short as a few days for hot new products or for physicians who are high-volume prescribers.

A congenial, positive attitude is a must if you're to make a memorable impression on your contacts and acquire new customers. Once a consistent client base is established, the constant drive to produce new business eases—although it's always an active part of a sales rep's daily functions, to some degree. Prospective client doctors are identified through a tracking system based on the prescriptions they write.

Landing one of these jobs usually takes either a science background or some sales experience. Of the two, sales experience is decidedly more important.

Salespeople who represent drugs that require a prescription are involved in what is called *indirect*, or *soft*, sales: The doctors don't actually buy anything from the rep. Rather, it's the sales rep's job to educate and raise awareness around his or her product as a means of influencing prescription orders, which lead to purchases by doctors' patients, at the pharmacy. Accordingly, these reps don't receive direct commissions; instead, they are eligible for quarterly or yearly bonuses based on exceeding sales objectives for an assigned territory.

Big Pharma companies have huge staffs of sales reps, so these positions can offer the necessary prerequisite for the more complex job of biotechnology sales, where salaries are higher and bonuses can exceed base salary.

Biotech Sales Representative

Biotech sales is more intensive, since the products can be a hundred times more costly than the typical pharmaceutical drug. You need an interest in science to be able to discuss the products, but medical-business savvy is crucial. Biotech sales reps advise physicians on insurance reimbursement issues and the logistics of delivering the drug to patients. Consider the case of a pediatrician contemplating a $5,000 product. Salaries for pediatricians are on the lower end of the MD scale, so a five-dose purchase can run them a significant percentage of their annual salary. One insider describes the situation like this: "If the insurance company doesn't pay for it, that's a large expense. We have to have people who will hold the doctor's hand. We'll help qualify the patient [make sure she fits the protocol for insurance reimbursement], and we have programs to help the doctor with cash flow."

Biotech sales reps operate with more autonomy and less support from a sales manager. The pressure can be great. "In pharma, you're evaluated on the activity you generate, the number of calls, your selling skills," says an insider. "Here [in a biotech company] we never talk about that. You either get it [the sale] or you don't—and if you don't, you're out the door." But the rewards of biotech sales are as great as the risk. Base salaries and bonuses are greater than in pharma sales jobs, and stock incentives play a larger part.

JOB OUTLOOK

You can choose from many different areas within the pharmaceutical and biotech industry when cultivating a career. You may decide to focus on one of the Big Pharma companies. This will most likely mean covering a larger territory, but it will also translate into larger bonus opportunities. Or you may choose a smaller drug maker that requires less learning of product information and a more centralized client base. Something else to consider is the type of product you want to represent. The range is wide—everything from acne creams to medicines designed to decrease cholesterol.

Those with BS or MS degrees in chemistry, molecular biology, genetics, biochemistry, computer science, and physics can find an easy foothold in this industry, although many nonscience undergrads can break into pharmaceutical sales with as much ease as their science counterparts. Big Pharma companies hire a huge number of sales reps.

If you're interested in getting into pharmaceutical sales, be aware that many times field reps become pigeonholed and find it hard to switch to another field such as technology sales. The industry does offer many jobs for those interested: According to the BLS, employment in the biotech and pharmaceutical industries will increase at a faster rate than the average through 2012. So while Big Pharma is under attack for its pricing and patent practices, it's still among the most profitable industries in the United States.

Above all, those who choose to work in this industry enjoy the very real satisfaction of knowing that they are laboring to provide drugs that could make a radical difference in the lives of thousands, even millions, of people.

Technology

In the 1980s, when IBM went looking for an operating system for its first personal computer, it didn't turn to Microsoft first. Rather it went to Santa Cruz, California, in search of a small but then-renowned company. But, according to the story, the programmers were out surfing. So IBM tapped Bill Gates for its operating system instead. Twenty years later, the technology market has become one of the biggest drivers of venture capital investment and it creates a significant amount of wealth for its stockholders. Advances in technology have enabled companies to function with speed, accuracy, and privacy—all essential to their growth and productivity.

Today, technology plays an integral role in asset management, communication, and branding in every field. An Oracle database can contain taxonomists' specie information (e.g., a database of newts would contain all known species along with the history and habitat of each), bank records, or retail inventories. E-mail and instant messaging applications allow people and companies to exchange information quickly. Companies that fail to implement the latest technologies into their infrastructures risk losing their competitive edge.

INDUSTRY OVERVIEW

The tech industry has witnessed many ups and downs since its boom in the 1990s and bust in the early 2000s. Stock prices that once soared to unbelievable heights—and investors' delight—would soon fall, leaving many bemoaning their misfortune. In the hardware sector, the demand for computers of all flavors, from servers to PCs, evaporated as companies around the world found themselves with excess computer hardware and cash-strapped consumers became reluctant to buy or upgrade PCs. However, home users turned the tide in 2003–04, buying powerful new machines to handle photo, video, and other demanding applications. PC shipments were up almost 15 percent in

2004. Now businesses are expected to take up the slack as they enter the midpoint of a hardware replacement cycle. The demand for more complex software systems is also on the rise, especially with so many services operating online. From banking to shopping, the need to protect personal information is greater than ever.

Technology sales—also referred to as IT (information technology), IS (information services), or enterprise technology sales—generally comprises two components: hardware and software sales. Traditional technology sales reps usually work in one of the two areas.

Hardware products comprise actual computer parts such as servers, mainframes, cables, routers, and modems that are purchased and integrated into the technology structure of a company. Software products are those applications that serve a specific function and are mapped on computer code to conduct or facilitate business processes.

INDUSTRY SECTORS

Computer Hardware

Computer hardware, as we use the term, means central processing units (CPUs), including memory and storage—in other words, the machine on which you run an operating system and application software and to which you attach peripherals (keyboard, mouse, printer, etc.). Also included in our definition are the servers, electronic security, and storage devices used in the data centers of many corporations.

The competition among computer hardware companies is particularly intense. On the one hand, in the traditional-PC market, companies' products have largely become commodified, with constant downward price pressure (and narrowing profit margins) being the result. On the other hand, there are the markets for innovative new products, like tablet PCs and ultra-minimal desktops, that are not yet fully commodified. Here, the race is to develop products at breakneck speed so you can be first to market. And if a company falters, it instantly becomes a target for larger companies looking to acquire new businesses. No doubt about it: Computer hardware is a cutthroat business.

There are definite geographic concentrations in the hardware industry despite its worldwide reach. It's often noted that high-tech companies are usually located near colleges and universities, and there's a good deal of truth to that, as many companies come out of research done at such institutions. Silicon Valley is near San Jose State, the University of California at Berkeley, and Stanford University. Route 128 is near the educational mecca of Cambridge, Massachusetts. Research Triangle in North Carolina and the area around Austin, Texas, are also good examples. Still, there are other places within North America where you'll find major companies; for example, Gateway is in North Dakota.

Most major corporations in computer hardware reach across national borders. International sales normally account for a large percentage of most hardware companies' bottom lines, and India, Japan, China, and other Asian locations are hotbeds of hardware manufacture and design.

The demands of this type of sales job vary widely depending on whether you are selling PCs or large servers and which markets you're selling into. In some instances, significant travel is required; in others, comparatively little. Training and support are usually provided so that you can learn your product's technical specifications as quickly and as thoroughly as possible.

Key Computer Hardware Manufacturers

Company	2004 Revenue ($M)	1-Year Change (%)	Employees
Hitachi, Ltd.	84,222*	3.4	306,876
Hewlett-Packard	79,905	9.4	151,000
Toshiba Corp.	52,816	11.9	166,651
Dell*	49,205	18.7	55,200
Fujitsu Limited	45,123	17.1	156,169
Canon	33,345	11.6	108,257
IBM Hardware	28,239	2.9	n/a
Cisco Systems	22,045	16.8	34,000
Ricoh Co.	16,852	16.2	73,137
Xerox Corp.	14,788	0.6	58,100
Seiko Epson Corp.	13,378	21.2	84,899
Sun Microsystems	11,185	−2.2	35,000
Apple Computer	8,279	33.4	13,426
EMC Corp.	8,230	32.0	22,700
Konica Minolta Holdings	8,145	74.6	20,523
Acer	7,036	52.2	6,560
Seagate Technology	6,224	−4.0	40,000
NCR Corp.	5,984	6.9	28,500
Lexmark International	5,314	11.8	13,400
Pitney Bowes	4,957	8.3	35,183

*2005 figures.
Sources: Hoover's; WetFeet analysis.

Computer Software

Computer software products accomplish discrete tasks and are sold as complete packages. Some computer software products are so-called applications, such as word processing and Web browsing. Computer software also includes operating systems, such as Windows, and utilities.

Most software purchases are made by businesses seeking better tools to manage the complexities of running operations, record keeping, and controlling the flow of money in and out of an enterprise. It's not always the quality of the code that determines what is the most successful software, but how well that software meets an actual business need. Probably the quickest way to talk yourself out of a job in this segment is to make the technology seem more important than the end user.

Much of the activity in computer software is happening in Silicon Valley, but you also might check out opportunities in other high-tech regions including Boston, Austin, Minneapolis, New York City, Denver, Dallas, Atlanta, Boca Raton, and the Research Triangle region of North Carolina.

Key Computer Software Companies

Company	2004 Revenue ($M)	1-Year Change (%)	Employees
Microsoft Corp.	36,835	14.4	57,000
IBM Software	15,094	5.5	n/a
SAP AG	10,179	15.3	32,802
Oracle Corp.	10,156	7.2	41,658
SunGard Data Systems	3,556	20.3	13,000
Computer Associates International	3,276	5.1	15,300
Electronic Arts	2,957	19.1	4,800
Konami Corp.	2,587	22.6	11,047
DST Systems	2,429	40.8	11,000
Thomson Learning*	2,052	−10.4	9,100
Veritas Software Corp.	2,042	16.9	7,587
Symantec Corp.	1,870	32.9	5,300
Intuit	1,868	18.1	6,700
SEGA Corp.	1,810	10.0	10,760
Amdocs Limited	1,774	19.6	10,600
Adobe Systems	1,667	28.7	3,142
Misys	1,651	−0.7	6,443
SAS Institute	1,530	14.2	9,528
BMC Software	1,419	6.9	6,429
Siebel Systems	1,340	−1.1	5,032

*2003 figures.
Sources: Hoover's; WetFeet analysis.

INDUSTRY TRENDS

Consolidation

Consolidation of the computer hardware sector makes sense as computers become familiar products that require fewer very different design and manufacturing approaches. Let a few giant companies manufacture more units at lower cost while sharing marketing and distribution costs across a larger organization. Hewlett-Packard came home with Compaq for billions, and rumor has it that Gateway is a prime takeover target.

The software sector has also been teeming with M&A activity. In 2004, Oracle spent $10.3 billion buying PeopleSoft, which had acquired business software maker J.D. Edwards the previous year. Earlier, Business Objects purchased Crystal Decisions, Hyperion Solutions bought Brio, and EMC bought Documentum and VMware. The reason for all of this activity: Buying competitors is a good way to increase market share—and buying them now, toward the beginning of an expected economic recovery, is smarter than buying them after their stock prices have risen too high.

Corporate Computing, Which Way?

One-stop-shopping versus best-of-breed? Which way to go is still up in the air while large software companies with these opposing product strategies continue to compete. Oracle and other enterprise software providers such as SAP believe companies want all of their software—from human resources tools to manufacturing planning—from a single source. Meanwhile IBM's strategy of acting as a high-level consultant drawing from a vast menu of software partners assumes that customers' needs are too diverse and switching costs too high for companies to trust their software functions to a single vendor.

SALES ROLE

Technology Sales Representative

The main role of a technical rep is to control a sales cycle from start to finish. This includes first prospecting and qualifying potential sales opportunities. Does your technology meet a client's specific needs? Who is the best contact within the company? HR, sales, manufacturing, and marketing each use technical products on a daily basis, but their specific needs will vary. Once you know the organizational structure of a company, such as who the key decision-makers are and whether they have an available budget, you're ready to make contact. Most large companies provide outline documents that walk their sales reps step-by-step through the process of qualifying a prospect customer. Every sales cycle or deal can range in possible revenue from thousands to many millions of dollars depending on the need. For example, huge data warehousing needs could mean that a company will have to spend as much as $50 million on one product. The larger the sale, the larger the possible commission. This is why sales careers in the tech industry are so appealing and competitive.

The tech sales rep has had to evolve over the past decade with a dramatically growing market. The players involved in the sales game have also changed, with increasingly more niche venders serving goliaths such as IBM. Many times these companies build strong relationships with single providers, making it difficult for sales reps from competing companies to get a foot in the door. That said, marketing plays a key role in building awareness of new and improved tech products. In fact, in most companies that produce computer software and hardware, it's the marketing department that calls the shots. Accordingly, sales and marketing divisions must work closely together to understand and meet the needs of their audience.

In addition, reps now not only have to effectively present their product, they also have to prove their company's overall stability. This means citing references, touting market leadership, and boasting financial strength within the market. With so much competition in the field, sales reps have to modify their selling process to make the big sales and high commissions that were once much easier to access. However, the aggressiveness required to close deals allows successful tech reps to cross into other areas of the industry more easily when advancing along their career paths.

To be a successful tech sales rep, you must be able to operate under stressful conditions and have the vision to see the bigger picture, that is, where the industry is heading. Having strong executive or C-level contacts (i.e., CEO, CFO), business savvy, and a competitive spirit will also effectively arm you to compete in this highly competitive field.

Technology Sales Audience

The demands of this job vary widely depending on the product you sell—for example large servers vs security software—and the markets you serve. Both hardware and software reps are in the business of "hard" sales, which means they have a direct impact on whether a company decides to buy a product or service. Technology sales comprises a tight field of competitors, with large and small companies competing for the same accounts.

Most purchases are made by businesses seeking better tools to manage the complexities of running operations, record keeping, and controlling the flow of money in and out of an enterprise. It's not always the quality of the code that determines what is the most successful software or hardware, but how well that technology meets an actual business need. Oftentimes, reps will call on customers with extensive technical backgrounds who can instantly spot faulty claims and uninformed reps. Sales representatives working in this field must become experts on their products. As such, ongoing training is a must to keep up with the latest trends in the industry.

JOB OUTLOOK

Owing to the technical expertise required for a technology sales position, job opportunities should remain plentiful. In fact, a 2004–05 BLS report claims that the software publishing industry is the fastest growing sector of the economy, predicted to grow by more than 68 percent by 2012. However, job seekers should not expect the high salary base once offered in the technology boom of the 1990s. While employers are constantly looking to hire competent sales reps, with specialized expertise and strong people skills, the competition to work at top companies such as Microsoft and Oracle remains strong.

Following the latest trends in the tech industry is the best path to landing a job. Companies experiencing rapid growth due to demand for their products must hire new reps for inside and outside sales. In the hardware industry, the trend toward wireless products is growing; whereas, the software industry is seeing more demand for security products to prevent identity and data theft.

The tech sales rep is a salaried position with compensation ranging from $25,000 to $105,000. Most positions also offer bonuses and commissions as a large part of the compensation.

Financial Services

When you think of financial services, most of us think about banking jobs—commercial banking posts like lending officers, or investment banking jobs like corporate finance analysts or traders. But there are a host of other opportunities in financial services, in companies of every size and culture imaginable—from small Internet start-ups to global financial powerhouses. No matter what your background, if you're smart and driven, there's likely a place for you.

Financial services is one of the fastest growing branches in the field of sales. With more and more people turning to financial advisors to help manage their personal wealth and prepare for the future, the need for strong financial experts is on the rise. Given the sprawling nature of this sector, this Insider Guide focuses on the money management aspect of financial services

When we think of those involved in the money management game, the title of broker and investment banker soon come to mind, but just as there are varying degrees of clients from every financial class, there are also numerous titles to work under when seeking a sales-related job in financial services. Two of the most sought-after positions in this field are in the areas of asset management and financial planning. To build a career in asset management, you'll need expert analytical skills and a real feel for the markets—as you pick a fund's securities, plot its strategy, and stay as close as possible to its objective. For those hoping to tap into the growing field of financial planning, knowledge of current tax laws and different investment strategies is a must. Whether you decide to be an independent or join a firm, there are many opportunities for those with sharp minds and strong people skills.

INDUSTRY OVERVIEW

More people invest in securities today than ever before, and not only are there more investments to choose from, including stocks, bonds, real estate investment trusts, limited partnerships, and an ever-growing diversity of mutual funds, there are also more ways to invest: via full-service brokerages, discount brokerages, and electronic trading for most of us as well as exclusive opportunities such as hedge funds and venture capital funds for high-net-worth individuals and institutional investors, such as pension funds, insurance companies, and university endowments. There's an unimaginably large amount of money chasing investments these days, which is one reason that the BLS reports this as a growing industry.

Agents who focus on the sale of securities and commodities are often referred to as *brokers*, *stockbrokers*, or *account executives*. Their primary function is to help customers design and manage a financial portfolio of investments. Stockbrokers may also work directly with other sales agents who are on the floor of the NYSE, where security purchase prices are negotiated and sold at breakneck speed. A broker must be very knowledgeable about the latest trends, often giving clients advice or explaining the intricacies of the trading market in great detail.

Those involved in financial services sales often focus more on the long-term financial planning of their clients. They focus on the sales of products associated with banking-related services such as retirement savings and insurance protection. These agents are referred to as *financial sales representatives* and *financial advisors*, and their main clientele are people with varying degrees of wealth.

INDUSTRY SECTORS

Brokerage

Retail brokerage firms allow individuals from all walks of life to ride the wild roller coaster that is the stock market. Retail brokerages make money primarily through commissions on the trades of their clients, though brokerage firms are trying to move their customers to fee-based management. The retail brokerage industry includes not only full-service brokers but also a number of discount and online brokers as well as the rarefied realm of private client services or private banking.

With more people becoming do-it-yourself investors, the role of the traditional broker is quickly becoming obsolete. But there are still clients who use brokers as the intermediaries between the buyer and seller in a securities transaction. The buyer and seller, not the brokerage firm, assume the risk. (If the firm acts as the principal or dealer, it deals from its own account and assumes some of the risk itself.) Brokers charge their clients a commission. A full-service firm such as Merrill Lynch charges commissions of up to several hundreds of dollars for transactions, and in return offers extras such as tailored research, strategy and planning, and asset management accounts—checking, credit (including lending on margin), and brokerage, all in one convenient package. A discount broker, such as TD Waterhouse, generally executes trade orders and issues a confirmation with few or no frills.

"" Acquiring new clients is really based on trust. Savvy people with money to invest don't want to just work with people who are smart. They want someone they can trust to help them connect the dots toward financial security and success.

Frills or no frills, to be authorized to trade on the various exchanges, you need to be a registered representative and licensed by the National Association of Securities Dealers.

Top Retail Brokerage Companies

Firm	2004 Client Assets ($M)	1-Year Change (%)	Revenue ($M)	Employees
Merrill Lynch GPC	1,400,000	9	9,831	n/a
Smith Barney (Citigroup)	978,000	7	6,500	n/a
Charles Schwab	733,000	8	4,188	14,200
Wachovia Securities	652,500	13	4,400	19,000
Morgan Stanley	602,000	7	4,615	n/a
Fidelity Personal Investments	588,300	40	n/a	n/a
UBS Financial Services	533,968	4	4,256	17,388
Edward Jones	357,000	43	2,891	31,400
A.G. Edwards	312,000	26	2,608	15,390
TD Waterhouse Investor Services	172,300	−2	n/a	n/a
Bank of America Investment Services	149,000	67	n/a	4,000
Raymond James & Associates	136,000	36	1,829	n/a
E-Trade	88,100	24	924	3,320
Ameritrade	79,900	23	922	1,961
Piper Jaffray	51,000	2	355	3,027
American Express Financial Advisors	n/a	n/a	7,035	n/a

Notes: E-Trade revenue and assets for brokerage segment, staff for entire firm; Schwab figures exclude institutional business; Edward Jones data is from parent, The Jones Financial Companies; UBS revenue is operating income. Sources: WetFeet analysis; Hoover's; SEC EDGAR Database.

Mutual Funds

Whereas brokers act on investors' orders, mutual fund managers raise cash from shareholders and then invest it in stocks, bonds, money-market securities, currencies, options, gold, or whatever else seems likely to make money. Mutual funds often have a specific investment focus—whether it's income, long-term growth, small cap, large cap, or foreign companies. And managers are restricted in the kinds of investments they can make. Compared to individual portfolios, funds hope to persuade investors that they offer several advantages: professional money management, liquidity, and more diversification than most individuals can create or afford in a personal portfolio, particularly now that switching between funds is allowed.

All investors share equally in the gains and losses of a fund, and the most important factor in choosing one—whether to work for or invest in—is probably your tolerance for risk. Bull markets tend to make many funds look good, but a downward turn or a jump in interest rates can have a significant negative impact that may take longer to correct for a fund than for the nimble independent investor's portfolio.

INDUSTRY TRENDS

Commissions to Fees

The retail brokerage industry is weaning itself from its traditional reliance on trade-based commissions by offering increasingly more fee-based services, which provide a more regular revenue stream in a volatile market. The fee structure also helps insulate firms from appearing to have conflicts of interest. Since the fee is usually a percentage of assets under management, it's in everyone's interest to see those assets grow. To give you a measure of this trend, fees represented approximately 25 percent of revenues in 2003, compared to less than 10 percent at the beginning of the decade; fees are expected to account for more than 40 percent of revenues in 5 years.

Dude, Where's My Brokerage?

During the trading frenzy of the late '90s, virtual brokers such as E-Trade and Ameritrade were the vehicles of choice for the savvy day trader, but with many of those folks now eating Ramen noodles, these companies have experienced serious declines in activity. Investors increasingly appear to want experienced advice and are willing to pay reasonable incremental costs for help in navigating the current turbulent markets. Though the market rebounded in 2004, retail brokerages have focused on keeping a neat bottom line and have resisted aggressive hiring. This is due in no small part to the costs associated with training new brokers—analysts estimate that a full-service brokerage pays about $250,000 to train a new broker and that even seasoned brokers cost firms $150,000 a year.

The strategy most firms have adopted to cope with this fact is consolidation. Wachovia and Prudential joined forces, creating the third-largest retail brokerage in terms of brokers and customer assets in 2003. In 2002, Ameritrade Holdings purchased Datek Online. Most recently, Bank of America purchased Fleet and its brokerage subsidiary, Quick & Reilly. Dozens of regional brokerages are merging as well, in hopes that lashing themselves together will keep them from breaking up in the current economic maelstrom.

SALES ROLES

Financial Sales Representative or Account Executive

Over the last 5 years, the financial services market, which once offered 20 to 30 percent returns on investments over short periods, has taken a dive. Now with more people turning to long-term financial planning over short-term investing, financial sales reps have been forced to make huge shifts in their current role. In the past, most financial sales reps were distinguished by the product they sold, whether it was securities or insurance annuities, and they typically made most of their earnings collecting transactional fees. In today's market, selling financial products is just a part of a financial sales rep's responsibility, whereas managing the money of long-term clients has taken center stage. Now, with recent government deregulations within the industry, agents often sell overlapping products, which translates into increased competition in the marketplace. Acquiring new clients is really based on trust.

Those starting out in the business usually take positions within investment companies in what is referred to as a tiered system.

P1: Platform 1 Reps

Platform 1, or P1, financial reps are considered employees of a large company that offers financial services to individuals and large businesses. As a financial rep at this level, you may manage the finances of various individual clients or institutional investors such as banks. For those representing more affluent individual clients, the title of private banker may be applied.

Working for a company has the benefit of established marketing and services training programs along with structured systems for acquiring new clients. Some companies go as far as supplying their sales reps with continuous leads. Reps must also adhere more closely to company policies and procedures when working with clients.

P1 reps usually receive a base salary plus commission for product sales.

Since the field is so competitive, there's a large fallout ratio for starting reps. It takes an average of 5 to 6 years for new financial reps to establish themselves in the field.

P2: Platform 2 Reps

Those who do succeed often opt to move on to the second tier or P2, which involves becoming a franchisee of a major company such as American Express. These sales reps work on 100 percent commission and pay a franchise fee to work under a larger company's umbrella. Unlike P1 reps, P2 reps don't have to follow the policies and procedures of the company and can serve their clients with sole discretion. Many make their earning through consolidated fees charged to their clients for long-term financial planning services.

Asset Manager

Asset mangers most often work for a branch, office, or department of a company or for high-net-worth individuals. Most private wealth management firms require a large minimum investment, typically at least $1 million. Elite firms such as JPMorgan often require investments of $5 million or more. Unlike financial advisors who service a broader public, asset managers must be aware of complex tax and legal structures for accounts and risk and return tradeoffs for numerous asset classes. Their focus is on larger portfolio administration and generation of return on investments. Those with individuals as clients must also deal with inheritance, tax, and legal issues.

Most individuals hoping to break into asset management have an MBA or a CPA license. To be an asset manager, you'll also need to pass the Series 7 exam required for registration. The Chartered Financial Analyst (CFA) designation is another huge plus for those planning to enter this field.

JOB OUTLOOK

Financial services sales positions are forecast as one of the strongest areas for job growth in the next 5 to 10 years.

People in sales no longer focus on just funds for investment. They need to be able to sell any one of a growing spectrum of financial products, depending on a customer's short- and long-term needs—and whatever his sister-in-law told him to do last week. Marketers focus on both the long-term picture and specific current product offerings. Who needs what and how much will they pay for it? Not only will you be expected to provide quality products, but also sound investment advice, help with estate planning, and retirement funds. As one insider says, "Acquiring new clients is really based on trust. Savvy people with money to invest don't want to just work with people who are smart. They want someone they can trust to help them connect the dots toward financial security and success."

The financial services market is a very competitive field with work taking place in high-stress situations. When the market is up, reps are viewed as heroes. But when it's down, they are often the first ones to take the heat from anxious clients. And although most financial reps are considered employees of large firms, the pressure to build a solid client base is great and may include cold-calling, individual advertising, social networking, and if you're lucky, inheriting clients from retiring reps.

The starting annual salary for this position can be as low as $21,000 before commissions and can move up to a more standard $140,000 once you're established. Bonuses can augment these figures significantly, particularly if you and your firm do well. The top 15 to 20 percent earn more than $250,000; an increasing number of these overachievers are in their 30s and 40s.

Insurance

Insurance may not strike you as the sexiest of industries, but there's a steady demand for its products—and it's a good industry if you're looking for a relatively stable career. Similar to financial services, but with more insurance protection products, insurance companies offer personal and commercial lines including basic health/life and property/casualty protection as well as a long list of other coverage types ranging from automobile to mortgages to insurance for insurance companies (known as *reinsurance*). These products protect customers from losses resulting from illegal actions, medical needs, theft, earthquakes and hurricanes, and a variety of other causes.

INDUSTRY OVERVIEW

Insurance companies calculate the likely cost of a given loss, divide it by the number of people who want protection against it, add in a little extra for profit, and reach an amount that they charge each customer for a policy guaranteeing compensation should the loss occur. But that's only the beginning. Insurance companies also mount huge marketing campaigns to convince customers that they need protection in general and the company's products in particular.

They also function as financiers, deriving a large part of their revenues from investments. Insurance companies must maintain enormous reserves of capital to back up potential claims obligations. They invest those reserves in stocks, bonds, and real estate, in the United States and overseas, providing an enormous amount of liquidity to financial markets and giving the industry an influence on the national economy far out of proportion to its size.

INDUSTRY SECTORS

Life and Health Insurance

The policies in this sector provide benefits packages that policyholders pay a premium to enjoy. Health insurance has gone through some major overhauls, including the replacement of fixed-fee Blue Cross/Blue Shield–inspired policies with managed care networks. The life insurance business is experiencing slow growth, and life insurance companies are likely to be merging with banks and securities firms. Hartford, Prudential, and MetLife are U.S. leaders in the life insurance game, while Aetna and CIGNA rule the HMO realm.

Property and Casualty Insurance

The focus of property and casualty insurance is on protection for owners of cars, homes, and businesses from loss, damage, and injury. Competition is fierce in this sector, and profits are falling. Only the strong will survive as weaker companies continue to tank and even more secure ones sell off this line.

Reinsurance

In the simplest terms, reinsurance is the insurance of insurance companies. Insurance companies pay reinsurers to assume some or all of the risk the insurers have taken on in writing policies for their clients. Insurers use reinsurance to protect against the risk of unusual losses. Reinsurers write reinsurance because their business allows them to pool enormous numbers of individual insurance risks, making their risks even more predictable than the risks faced by primary insurers.

Key Insurance Companies

Company	2004 Revenue ($M)	1-Year Change (%)	Employees
AXA	132,547	6.6	74,584*
Allianz AG	129,536	1.4	162,180
ING Groep N.V.	115,324	8.3	113,039
American International Group	97,987	20.5	92,000
Nippon Life Insurance Co.	68,261	9.7	70,073
Prudential plc	59,685	13.9	21,500
State Farm Mutual Automobile Insurance Co.*	56,100	12.9	79,000
MetLife	39,014	9.0	54,000
Aegon N.V.	38,624	7.2	27,446
The Allstate Corp.	33,936	5.7	39,400
Swiss Reinsurance Co.*	31,888	8.7	8,359
Prudential Financial	28,348	1.6	39,418
New York Life Insurance Co.*	25,700	4.0	12,100
The St. Paul Travelers Companies	22,934	159.0	30,200
The Hartford Financial Services Group	22,693	21.1	30,000
Massachusetts Mutual Life Insurance Co.*	17,947	10.4	10,000
Nationwide Mutual Insurance Co.*	16,803	−42.9	30,000
Liberty Mutual Insurance Co.*	16,618	14.3	38,000
The Northwestern Mutual Life Insurance Co.*	16,545	3.3	4,500
Loews Corp.	15,242	−7.4	22,000

*2003 figures.
Sources: Hoover's; WetFeet analysis.

INDUSTRY TRENDS

Terrorism and Insurance

After 9/11, insurance companies were faced with tremendous claims, which led reinsurers to stop writing terrorism policies in the United States. As a result, primary insurers started stripping terrorism coverage out of policy renewals in states where doing so was legal and stopped offering or renewing policies that included terrorism insurance in states where it was not. In response, the Bush administration stepped into the picture with the Terrorism Risk Insurance Act of 2002, which acts as a kind of safety net for writers of commercial insurance. The Act requires insurers to pay terrorism-related claims up to a ceiling; beyond that ceiling, the government will pay the bulk of claims, thus limiting the insurance industry's risk exposure. Set to expire in 2005, legislation that would extend the Act for 2 more years and establish a commission to develop a long-term plan for terrorism insurance was pending at press time.

Changing the Face of Insurance

Deregulation has been redefining what companies can offer as insurance since the repeal of the 1933 Glass-Steagall Act in 1999. (Glass-Steagall formerly separated all arenas of financial services.) As a consequence, insurers, banks, and securities brokers can merge and cross-sell each others' products, with insurance companies offering investment and savings options as well as insurance and commercial banks offering products previously only available from traditional insurance companies.

Meanwhile, demand for products is extending beyond life insurance to new types of products, such as annuities, which provide customers with regular payments for life or for a fixed period. As a consequence, insurers have been shifting their capabilities from analyzing and predicting mortality rates to investment-management capabilities. In a creative move, insurers are building a market for products that protect the investor against a variety of risks while allowing them to draw down a death benefit while still alive.

SALES ROLE: INSURANCE AGENT OR BROKER

Think of being an agent and broker as giving advice for a living. You'll tell others how they can best protect their valuables. Then you'll sell them a policy.

Your aunt may forget to send you a birthday card, but you can be sure that your insurance agent won't, because a strong client-to-agent relationship is what makes an insurance agent successful. A college degree is not a requirement to be an agent, though many agents are college grads. What is required are strong communication skills, the ability to multitask, and an expert knowledge of your product line. Knowledge of insurance contracts is essential.

Most insurance agents work out of an office whether they work alone or with a group of other agents representing the same company. Those agents who only represent one company are called *captive agents*, whereas independent agents who provide services from multiple suppliers are often called simply *agents* or *brokers*. Insurance reps aren't required to do a significant amount of travel unless visiting commercial clients such as small businesses or when asked to validate claims in person.

Most states require agents take mandatory courses and pass state exams before they can practice. This means obtaining specific state licenses with the need of additional ones in the designated areas of health, property, and casualty insurance. And those agents wishing to also provide securities and financial products to their customers must also take steps established by the National Association of Securities Dealers that include specific exam and licensing requirements.

Advances in technology have decreased demand for agents and brokers, owing to the accessibility of insurance products online, but that have has also allowed agents to widen their customer base. For example, software now allows for faster loan processing and data tracking.

JOB OUTLOOK

The insurance industry enjoys more demand for its products today than ever before. As the U.S. population grows and Baby Boomers age, demand fore health insurance, auto insurance, and homeowners insurance will be especially strong.

However, ongoing consolidation and technological advances make it unlikely that job opportunities in many functional areas will grow at a strong rate in the insurance industry. The BLS projects 8 percent growth for the industry between 2002 and 2012, half of the 16 percent job growth rate that is the average for all industries combined.

When companies combine, redundant positions tend to be eliminated. And as interactions with insurance clients, as well as internal business processes, become increasingly automated, demand will decrease for employees in roles increasingly replaced by new technologies; insurance agents and underwriters are expected to be most negatively affected by the increasing role of technology in the industry.

Job opportunities in some functional roles in the industry are expected to grow, however. In addition, agents who can sell a variety of types of insurance or financial services will face much better prospects than traditional insurance agents. The salary range is $30,000 to $50,000 or more depending on the size and type of client base.

Manufacturing

Manufacturing is a broad term. Virtually any process that turns raw material into a finished product through use of a machine can be considered manufacturing. If you look around at the objects strewn about the room in which you're currently sitting, you'll see that quite a few things are manufactured. Many of these products will come from well-known names such as General Mills and PepsiCo while others were produced in the private sector by small companies with unfamiliar names. And because manufacturers come in a variety of sizes, the salespeople who bring their products to the market are a diverse lot, from sales reps who work as employees for single companies to independent contractors who oversee the sales needs of multiple manufacturers at once.

For those wishing to pursue a career in product sales, understanding the different tiers of the industry is crucial. Most sales positions for manufactured goods come from the public sector of big consumer product companies such as Procter & Gamble. These sales professionals are referred to as *consumer sales reps.* However, there are many manufacturers with products to sell in the private sector as well. Often these smaller companies will outsource their sales work to independent contractors, called *manufacturer reps,* to limit their costs.

INDUSTRY OVERVIEW

Consumer products are the foundation of the modern consumer economy. The industry itself not only generates an enormous portion of the gross domestic product, it also pumps huge amounts of money into other industries, notably advertising and retail. Individual consumers make up the majority of this industry's customers; sales are concentrated in the United States, Japan, and Western Europe, though other parts of the world are working hard for the privileges of wearing clothing emblazoned with company logos, eating processed food, and chopping vegetables with an electric motor instead of a traditional utensil. Success in consumer products is all about marketing an individual product, often by promoting a brand name. The competition is ferocious for shelf space, so package design, marketing, and customer satisfaction are key elements.

In addition to the consumer goods industry dominated by companies such as Nestle and Unilever, the universe of manufacturing also expands to include companies manufacturing a spectrum of products—from aerospace and defense, automobile and transportation, chemicals and metals, to electronics and high-tech, industrial and farm, and medical and biotech products. Generally, sectors that involve technology and are less mature—especially biotech and medical manufacturing—represent high-growth opportunities, whereas those that have reached maturity—chemical and metals, for instance—are waning and have seen much of their growth exported overseas.

INDUSTRY SECTORS

Consumer Products

The consumer products industry, represented by consumer sales reps working solely for large companies, can be divided into four sectors: beverages; foods; toiletries, cosmetics, and cleaning products; and small appliances. Many companies operate in only one category—especially smaller companies. Others, including many of the big dogs of the industry, are what are commonly called *diversified CPG* companies: They make and sell products in multiple categories. Nestlé's brands, for instance, include products in the food (e.g., Toll House cookies), beverage (Nestea), and pet care (Alpo) categories. In many cases, diversified CPG companies started out by making products in just one category, but diversified over time via mergers and acquisitions.

Virtually all companies in the industry are similar in their organizational structure, emphasis on brand management, and approach to business.

Beverages. Intensely competitive and hugely reliant on advertising, this is a mature sector. Different segments of the beverage world include beer (Adolph Coors, Anheuser-Busch, Miller, Stroh's), soft drinks (Coca-Cola, PepsiCo), and juices (Tropicana is owned by PepsiCo, Minute Maid by Coca-Cola).

Foods. There may be a little less consolidation in the foods sector than in beverages, but this is also a mature and competitive sector with single-digit growth. Most of the packaged goods that fill our pantries, cupboards, and refrigerators come from a handful of big-league corporate players. Some are household names: Campbell Soup, General Mills, H.J. Heinz, and Kellogg have spent enormous sums of money to imprint their names on your brain. Other big players, such as ConAgra are better known for brands they own: Hunt's, Healthy Choice, and Wesson are all ConAgra brands.

Toiletries, cosmetics, and cleaning products. Baby Boomers aren't getting any younger, and vanity will outlast us all. So will household dirt. So this is a solid category for the foreseeable future. At 3½ times the size of its nearest competitor, Procter & Gamble is the Godzilla of this group—and indeed the consumer products world in general. Other players include Clorox, Colgate-Palmolive, Revlon, Gillette, Kimberly-Clark (maker of Huggies, Kotex, and Kleenex, among others), Unilever, and S.C. Johnson (Pledge, Glade, and Windex).

Small appliances. This is an amalgam of companies in various industries. More people are building and buying homes, and forecasters don't expect the trend to slow. So tools, kitchen gadgets, air conditioners, chain saws, and anything else Saturday shoppers enjoy pausing over in the hardware store are selling well, and the future looks rosy for this segment of the industry. Nevertheless, this is also a relatively mature industry, and the brand system is not as strong as it is in other categories. Players here include Black & Decker, Sears, and Snap-On.

Key Consumer Products Companies

Company	2004 Revenue ($M)	1-Year Change (%)	Employees
Nestlé S.A.	76,660	8.2	253,000*
Altria Group	63,963	5.4	156,000
Unilever	54,413	1.4	223,000
The Procter & Gamble Co.	51,407	18.5	110,000
Johnson & Johnson	47,348	13.1	109,900
Kraft Foods	32,168	3.7	98,000
PepsiCo	29,261	8.5	153,000
The Coca-Cola Co.	21,962	4.4	50,000
Sara Lee Corp.	19,566	7.0	150,400
L'Oréal SA	19,284	12.6	52,081
Wyeth	17,358	9.5	51,401
Emerson Electric Co.	15,615	11.9	107,800
Kimberly-Clark Corp.	15,083	5.1	60,000
Anheuser-Busch Cos.	14,934	5.6	31,435
ConAgra Foods	14,522	−26.8	39,000
GE Consumer & Industrial	13,767	7.2	75,000*
Whirlpool Corp.	13,220	8.6	68,000
SABMiller	11,366	37.0	39,571
General Mills	11,070	5.4	27,580
Colgate-Palmolive Co.	10,584	6.9	36,000

*2003 figures.
Sources: Hoover's; WetFeet analysis.

Other Manufacturing

Along with the large CPG companies are those manufacturers that produce products that range from the cars we drive to the plastic Tupperware that stores last night's leftovers. These manufacturers use a variety of sales tactics from employed reps to independent contractors, depending on their size and production infrastructure. Whether you are a car salesmen on a lot or the manufacturers rep stocking stores with less familiar brands of electronics, manufacturing offers a wide range of products to represent.

Automobiles and components. The leaders in this segment are the Big Three auto manufacturers: DaimlerChrysler, Ford, and General Motors. There are also foreign manufacturers producing autos in the United States, including Nissan, Honda, Toyota, and BMW. Auto manufacturing is one of the most global of the manufacturing sectors. For job seekers, it means potentially international clients especially when looking for smaller competitors in the industry to represent.

Chemicals and metals. Chemical and metal manufacturers tend to be process manufacturers; their production is characterized by long, continuous runs. Picture sheets of steel rolling continuously out of a furnace. Chemicals and metals provide the building blocks for a myriad of other products. Large manufacturers like Alcoa not only produce aluminum for your Coke can, but also for 747s. Most of the world's largest metal producers now reside overseas. As with the metals industries, chemicals in the United States are somewhat stagnant but also subjected to the vagaries of the oil market. Less susceptible to prices of oil and commodities are specialty chemical manufacturers— companies such as Eastman Chemical whose end products require more engineering and production effort than commodity chemicals.

Electronics. Electronics manufacturers (excluding high-tech/computer hardware, which are covered in the "Technology" industry profile earlier in this chapter) divide themselves into two camps, consumer electronics manufacturers and industrial manufacturers. The consumer camp is dominated by foreign firms, such as Sony and Matsushita

(Panasonic). This sector is, not surprisingly, closely tied to consumer spending and the overall health of the economy. And while everyone has a television and a CD player, the industry thrives on technological advances that create new markets.

Industrial and farm equipment. John Deere plowed the way for the industrial equipment industry with the invention of the steel plow that broke through the tough but fertile sod of the Great Plains. Today, industrial manufacturers make equipment for agriculture, construction, and mining as well as diesel engines for large trucks and generators. Since most new construction and mining projects are overseas, the larger companies within the industry have developed significant overseas operations.

Medical manufacturing. The medical manufacturing industry has the unique distinction of combining manufacturing technology with medicine. For those who go into the field, there's a large degree of satisfaction from the knowledge that you're doing something very good for mankind. The R&D process for medical manufacturing is more akin to that of pharmaceuticals than to industrial manufacturing. Product development includes huge development costs and a lengthy and costly FDA approval process. So, as with pharmaceuticals, a company's fortunes ride heavily on the will of the FDA. The largest companies in the industry include Johnson & Johnson, GE OEC Medical Systems, Baxter, Tyco Healthcare, Medtronic, and Boston Scientific.

Key Manufacturing Companies

Company	2004 Revenue ($M)	1-Year Change (%)	Employees
General Motors Corp.	193,517	4.3	324,000
DaimlerChrysler AG	192,433	12.2	384,723
Ford Motor Co.	171,652	4.5	324,864
Toyota Motor Corp.	163,637	26.9	264,410
General Electric Co.	151,300	13.9	307,000
Volkswagen AG	121,346	10.9	342,502
Samsung Group*	101,459	−16.7	195,000
Honda Motor Co.	78,222	15.9	131,600
Nissan Motor Co.	70,087	23.2	123,748
Bayerische Motoren Werke (BMW)	60,473	16.0	105,972
Robert Bosch GmbH	54,570	19.6	242,348
Boeing Co.	52,457	3.9	159,000
BASF AG	51,573	21.1	81,955
The Dow Chemical Co.	40,161	23.1	43,203
United Technologies Corp.	36,700	19.5	210,000
Lockheed Martin Corp.	35,526	11.6	130,000
Northrop Grumman Corp.	29,853	13.9	125,400
Delphi Corp.	28,622	1.9	185,200
ExxonMobil Chemical Co.	27,781	37.6	n/a
E. I. du Pont de Nemours and Co. (DuPont)	27,340	1.3	60,000

*2003 figures.
Sources: Hoover's; WetFeet analysis.

INDUSTRY TRENDS

Alliances

Many of the more forward-thinking CPG companies are trying to enhance growth via alliances with other companies. One CPG insider says of her company's partnership on a product line with a big industry competitor, "It seems amazing that we're partnering with 'the enemy,' but it's true." CPG companies are doing this for a number of reasons. Some are doing it to create and bring to market new products with less risk than they'd have if they were going it alone; for instance, PepsiCo and Starbucks teamed up to create a line of bottled coffee drinks. Some are doing it to reach new demographics; for example, Coca-Cola teamed with Danone to distribute bottled-water products to new customer segments. Others are doing it to expand geographically into new markets; General Mills, for instance, has joined forces with Nestlé to market breakfast cereals outside North America. And some do it for other reasons, such as to increase operating efficiencies, cut costs, or reduce capital outlays.

New Technologies

As in most industries these days, technology is becoming an ever more significant factor in doing business in the CPG industry. One of the biggest technology trends is the rise in importance of customer relationship management (CRM) applications. CRM software collects information about customers, their behavior, and all aspects of their relationship with a company, allowing the company to better understand the marketplace for its products and how to increase sales and market presence.

The Internet is another area of technology that's had a big impact on CPG marketing. In the Internet arena, the most successful companies are using the interactivity of the Web to strengthen the relationship between consumers and their brands. Campbell Soup, Coca-Cola, and Hershey's all offer online gift shops where Internet surfers can buy branded collectibles such as decorative tins, T-shirts, and plush toys.

Lean Manufacturing

Lean manufacturing was developed by Toyota and its Toyota Production System more than a decade ago. Traditional manufacturing methodologies stress high utilization of machinery with slim regard for cycle time or manufacturing waste. Lean manufacturing, on the other hand, stresses reduced cycle times and waste. *Cycle time* refers to the amount of time that it takes to complete a set of operations. So in lean manufacturing, the goal is not to push more goods through a process—say, the painting area of an automobile assembly line—but rather to develop a better process. Similarly, lean manufacturing attacks root causes by identifying "seven wastes": overproduction, transportation, motion, waiting, processing, inventory, and defects.

Expanded Outsourcing

Though contract manufacturing is not a new concept, its scope continues to increase. Companies such as Solectron and Flextronics already manufacture computers and electronics for better-known companies such as Hewlett-Packard, Cisco, and Apple. Now, however, these companies are seeking to expand by tapping new markets, such as consumer electronics and automobile parts, and adding supply chain and materials management services to their offerings. Within the automotive industry, companies such as BMW are already experimenting with outsourced production.

SALES ROLES

Consumer Sales Representative

You still see them from time to time, personable young people trundling from small retailer to small retailer promoting their wares. Sales is generally the easiest place to enter a consumer products company if you have little or no work experience. Those who become successful at this type of work are usually stronger on personality and gumption than on higher education. Generally, the bigger the accounts you work on, the more money you can make. At the senior level, the earning potential far surpasses that of a brand manager—and you won't have the MBA debt to worry about either.

Consumer sales is a starting point for many people beginning a career in sales. It's a great place to get experience without the major stress that comes with hard sales (where reps have a direct impact on sales) industries such as technology or financial services. As a consumer sales representative, you're responsible for the public's perception of your product on the shelves. Consumer sales reps not only develop strong relationships with retailers displaying their products, they also promote their companies' products to the general public with promotional displays and product care, which involves managing the shelf and display units within a set of customer stores. This includes restocking and rotating your product on a periodic schedule—often this requires heavy lifting (at least 32 pounds).

Because most sales reps have a consistent set of customers who also benefit by offering popular products, travel requirements and stress levels are not as high as in other sales jobs. That said, senior-level positions often handle larger accounts requiring more travel even as they are responsible for managing the product displays of their customers.

Manufacturer Representative

While most people have heard of consumer sales reps, discussed in the previous section, a sales position with less notoriety is that of the manufacturing sales rep who works on the behalf of smaller manufacturers instead of for large corporations. This is often the case for smaller manufacturers looking to cut costs by contracting out their sales needs. Manufacturing goods that are produced by companies without an intact sales team of their own will hire manufacturer reps as intermediaries between their clients, the manufacturers, and the retail arena that sells goods.

Those interested in becoming manufacturer reps have a wide assortment of companies from which to build a client base. Most manufacturer reps work within a specific industry as a way to narrow down not only their prospecting cycle but also the expertise they must possess. To be successful as a manufacturer rep, a thorough understanding of the intricacies of the products you represent is a must.

A manufacturer rep usually works a specific territory within a region of a state or country. The sales process is solely at the rep's discretion; he or she plans his or her own schedule and style of soliciting business. Frequently, this position requires cold-calling customers for initial contact with retail buyers and purchasing agents, in hopes of initiating long-lasting relationships. Over time, manufacturer reps will build a consistent client base. Manufacturer reps must become experts on the product they represent, able to answer customer questions and even provide training when needed. Their responsibilities may also include advising clients on ways to cut costs, increase sales, and stay competitive with product upgrades and marketing techniques.

With complex products involving technological advances, the sales reps will be responsible for connecting their customers with expert technicians within the company for further training. As the intermediary between the supplier and the customer, the manufacturer rep makes initial contact, presents products, and sets up relationships that allow products to make it to store shelves. They're responsible for follow-up visits to ensure that the customer is satisfied with the product and to address any concerns or problems that may arise.

Most manufacturer reps are self-employed and as such must possess basic business skills. To run a successful practice, manufacturer reps must keep abreast of the latest product trends, perform multiple administrative duties from accounting to scheduling, and maintain a consistent pipeline of future employees. Often, manufacturer reps must also travel to meet face-to-face with potential clients and companies here and abroad whose products they hope to represent.

JOB OUTLOOK

Consumer Products

The hiring outlook at CPG companies depends primarily on the financial performance of those companies. If a company is growing, it will be hiring. After a few years in the doldrums due to the recession in the early 2000s, CPG companies are starting to enjoy growth again. As a result, some companies are hiring. But by most accounts, the economy is not yet out of the woods. Therefore, even companies that are hiring are doing so cautiously.

The salary range for most consumer sales positions is $25,000 to $100,000, with potential bonuses for those who meet year quotas ahead of schedule or work on larger accounts with major distributors.

Other Manufacturing

To paraphrase Orwell, some manufacturing sectors are more equal than others. Mature industry segments have been exported overseas for many years. Overall, the manufacturing industry is not growing in the United States. Within the industry, many sectors, such as aerospace and defense and the automobile industry are undergoing continued consolidation. During the recent recession, companies have undertaken significant workforce reductions.

Bright spots abound, though, and they tend to be exceptionally bright. Areas such as medical manufacturing and specialty electronics manufacturing have been growing steadily. Moreover, they stand to show even more growth with coming advances in nanotechnologies.

Although the industry as a whole cannot be described as booming, the outlook is much more sanguine now than it has been for many years. Similarly, as the economy continues to gain strength, the industry will likely trend up along with it. For job seekers, especially recent college graduates, the outlook appears decent. The BLS reports that job growth for manufacturer representatives through the year 2012 is expected to match the average for job growth across all industries.

The best opportunities will be in small wholesale and manufacturing companies that need to hire independent sales reps to control costs. Manufacturing's diverse group of products, companies, and clients translates into average compensation that can range from $35,000 to $100,000 and above based on salary plus commission.

Real Estate

Everything we do, commercial and personal, real and virtual, requires space and therefore the land on which space sits. The real estate industry has taken this law of nature and run with it. The real estate industry is powered by agents who work in concert to make land available—physically, legally, and financially—for every imaginable human need.

Most agents working in the real estate field sell residential property including various single home listings in a town or city or as an agent working for a land developer selling pre-constructed homes in a planned community or vacation time shares. But there are also lucrative opportunities in other areas of real estate such as the sale of commercial, industrial, or agricultural property. As an agent you may choose to work for a large firm or as an independent contractor.

INDUSTRY OVERVIEW

Real estate brokerages match supply with demand; they bring together parties interested in selling, buying, leasing, or exchanging property. Real estate agents, who directly sell properties, must work under a broker and typically turn over a portion of their commission to the brokerage, or they can obtain the extra licensing necessary to become brokers themselves. Typically, brokers represent owners, buyers, or lessees, though firms rarely represent both buyer/tenant and seller/landlord in the same transaction. While residential brokers will represent both buying and selling parties, commercial brokers specialize in representing tenants, sellers, or buildings. Brokers split a fee ranging from 6 to 8 percent of the transaction. In both commercial and residential real estate, individual states require agents and brokers to obtain licenses to represent clients. Requirements for gaining credentials vary from state to state; however, the broker's license requires more education and work experience. Almost every state requires that agents practice under a broker.

Though most brokers and agents work for larger firms and thus benefit from their employers' support services and branding, they view themselves as independent businesses. Many brokerage companies offer only minimal benefits and put brokers on 100 percent commission-based compensation. The amount brokers earn depends on the market in which they operate. Brokers in markets with high real estate prices such as Manhattan and San Francisco tend to do much better than those in less-affected markets.

INDUSTRY SECTORS

In general, the real estate industry is highly fragmented. The largest companies in the industry garner only single-digit market share within their sectors. Centex, for example, one of the nation's largest homebuilders, controls less than 2 percent of the U.S. new housing market. And Sam Zell's Equity Office Properties, the largest real estate investment trust (REIT) in the country, controls only 2 percent of the country's office space. Because the market is so vast and because market knowledge doesn't transfer across regions, most companies tend to focus on segments of individual geographic markets. Homebuilders often focus on regions, such as the Southeast or Southwest—especially in the Sunbelt states where populations are growing, land is plentiful, and the building season is long. A REIT may be active in a particular market—retail, mall retail, office, warehouse, or investment residential—within a region. Smaller firms often operate within a single metropolitan area.

Because of this phenomenon, industry insiders usually spend much of their careers in the same geographic market. Though relocating doesn't necessarily mean starting from scratch, it does mean losing some of your accumulated social and intellectual capital of long-cultivated relationships and hard-won local knowledge.

Within the industry, a large chasm divides the commercial and residential sectors. Firms and individual agents involved in commercial real estate generally do not participate in the residential market and vice versa. This makes it difficult to leverage skills and experience when switching between sectors.

Residential Real Estate

Whether you work for a brokerage firm or as in individual agent, most work in the area of residential property. Residential real estate includes not only homes for single families and individuals but also the sale and purchase of multifamily dwellings, mobile homes, condominiums and townhouses, land for single residential construction, and small farms. Appreciation of home prices varies by geographic region. Agents working in rapidly appreciating markets on the East and West Coast enjoy shorter sales cycles and larger purchase prices than those working in Midwest sectors of the country. It is a very competitive market with many established agents dominating the field. Most agents work as independent contractors for smaller franchises such as Century 21, while others may choose to sell preconstructed homes for large developers such as KB Homes or for real estate companies that represent private investors looking to invest in residential real estate.

Those working in traditional residential real estate spend the majority of their time obtaining new clients through homeowners looking for help with the sale of their property. Contractual agreements with prospective sellers and buyers are formed in the way of a contract called a *listing*. Once signed by both parties, listings are legally binding. Good residential real estate agents have strong people skills and are willing to listen to the needs of their clients. Knowing the intricacies of various residential areas—such as the serving school districts, appreciation history of specific neighborhoods, and current tax laws—is a must.

Commercial and Industrial Real Estate

Commercial and industrial real estate involves the buying and selling of income-producing properties such as strip malls, industrial parks, apartment complexes, and warehouses. Although those working in this field can be independent contractors, most work as a member of a larger firm and specialize in specific types of properties such as retail centers. Commercial brokers typically represent tenants, sellers, or buildings. Successful agents not only track the local economic growth in their area, they must also stay abreast of tax laws that could affect the purchase of large commercial spaces. They must understand the needs of their clients, taking into consideration such issues as traffic patterns around retail complexes and the ease with which raw materials and finished goods can be transported to and from industrial sites.

Sales cycles are long in commercial real estate; a broker may work with a client for years before executing a transaction. "My last deal took 2½ years before we signed," says one insider. Moreover, commercial brokerage, as you might expect, is closely tied to the general business cycle.

Agricultural Real Estate

If you have ever watched the bucolic scenery roll by during a family trip, you have witnessed firsthand the large amounts of land required to keep the agricultural industry running. Real estate agents that buy and sell agricultural land are often referred to as *land brokers*. Their clients range from developers looking to acquire large rural areas for residential and commercial development to farming corporations looking to set up agricultural sites. In addition to the ability to estimate the profit potential of a piece of property, land brokers must possess knowledge of farming operations and environmental laws protecting rural stretches of land. Transportation issues, the cost of local utilities, and zoning regulations can all affect the sale of a piece of land. In this highly specialized field, which is often dominated by established agents and firms, agricultural transactions can turn huge profits due to the large amounts of acreage involved.

Key Real Estate Companies

Company	2004 Revenue ($M)	1-Year Change (%)	Employees
Cendant Corp.	19,785	8.8	87,000
Centex Corp.*	12,860*	24.1	17,134
Pulte Homes	11,711	29.4	13,000
D.R. Horton	10,841	24.2	7,466
Lennar Corp.	10,505	17.9	11,796
The Trump Organization	10,400	22.4	22,000
KB Home	7,008	21.3	6,000
Starwood Hotels & Resorts	5,368	42.0	120,000
NVR	4,250	15.6	4,407
Hovnanian Enterprises	4,160	29.9	3,837
M.D.C Holdings	4,009	37.3	3,600
The Ryland Group	3,952	14.7	2,829
Beazer Homes USA	3,907	23.0	3,428
Toll Brothers	3,862	40.0	4,655
Host Marriott	3,668	6.6	192
Standard Pacific	3,355	42.1	2,100
Equity Office Properties	3,305	−2.7	2,300
Simon Property Group	2,722	13.0	4,610
CB Richard Ellis Group	2,365	45.1	13,500
Tishman Realty & Construction	2,195	10.8	900

*2005 numbers.
Sources: *Fortune*; Hoover's; *Crain's New York Business*; WetFeet analysis.

INDUSTRY TRENDS

Wall Street Is Like Lithium

In former years, the real estate industry was like your brilliant but manic-depressive friend, with higher highs and lower lows. The cyclical nature of the industry was exacerbated by many small-time speculators who worked independently of one another. Developers tended to work with private capital and build on gut feel rather than sound analysis. The consequence was horrible overdevelopment during booms that led to overcapacity in lean years—a true boom-and-bust industry. As financial markets have taken over much of the financing of commercial development through REITs and private equity placement, they've also forced discipline on developers. Consequently, developers, now under Wall Street's scrutiny, have forced themselves to be much more disciplined—developments and property acquisitions are subject to sensitivity analysis and "what if" scenarios rather than wild hare speculation.

Cautious Gangbusters: The Outlook

First quarter 2005 housing starts surged, hitting an all-time high for single family homes and showing impressive results for the multifamily sector as well, driven by an improving rental market and strong growth in condo development. Sales of new and existing homes were also solid. All of this bodes well for the homebuilding industry after prognostications that 2005 wouldn't match the strength of 2004. Interest rates, which are moving upward, had been expected to create a drag on demand, but growth in the GDP—and rising employment and household income—are a promising offset. Buying by investors and speculators, and a rise in adjustable-rate mortgages, could complicate the picture, along with the acceleration in the growth of housing prices that have led some analysts to forecast the bursting of the housing bubble. There are other signs a slowdown may take place, though perhaps not until 2006. *Business Week* found that luxury homes declined in value in the last 3 months of 2004. A National Association of Realtors report that 36 percent of 2004's home sales were second homes, with 64 percent made as an investment, lends credence to the idea that the bubble may be getting bigger, however.

Commercial growth in 2005 promises an improvement over 2004, with multifamily dwellings expected to rise around 9 percent to $120 billion—topping the $112 billion spent at the peak of the dot-com boom in 2000. Expansion by retailers such as Lowe's and Wal-Mart, along with improving GDP, also bode well for the sector.

Office buildings appear to be rebounding as well, with the national vacancy rate dropping in 2004 and as much of 70 percent of new buildings being preleased. Conditions do, of course, vary depending on the market. In Riverside and San Bernardino, for instance, vacancy rates hit just 9.5 percent in early 2005—better than New York City. San Mateo, in Silicon Valley, still recovering from the dot-com implosion, was at 27 percent.

SALES ROLE: REAL ESTATE AGENT OR BROKER

To be an agent, you must be at least 18 years old and a high school graduate, and depending on the requirements of the state where you wish to practice, you must complete a course on real estate principles and two other areas of the industry. Some states require additional classroom training. Once you've successfully passed the required courses, you must pass a state exam. A commercial sales professional typically specializes in a specific property type: apartments, retail, office, commercial, and so on. To become a broker, you need an additional broker's license, which allows you to open your own agency.

In most states, real estate agents must work for a minimum of 2 years under the supervision of a broker before they can take the brokerage exam. This means that most agents act as independent contractors within a real estate firm owned by a broker. The broker charges agents a desk fee, which includes utilities and advertising expenses, and allows agents to use the main office as their own. Most agents with desk space receive an allotted amount of floor time, meaning all customers who walk into the office without already established relationships with another agent become the prospective client of the agent on the floor at the time. This is very important to new agents who are building a client base. There's also usually a commission structure between a broker and the agent. For beginner agents, it's usually as high as a 10/90 percent split, with agents taking the lower percentage until they've proven their skills and can renegotiate for a 50/50 percent split. Many franchises that take on first-time agents will provide in-house training on the selling process.

Brokers who are the lead agent on a sale often receive the full 100 percent of their commission. Some brokers, such as Century 21, own real estate franchises. Under that franchise they will hold the licenses of contracted agents, meaning that the broker is ultimately in charge of overseeing the sales process and is liable for any unethical practices involved. Often brokers who have been in the business for years do not sell themselves; instead they make their living off of the commission splits of the agents holding desk space within their firm.

The successful realtor is necessarily a savvy salesperson with a deep knowledge of real estate markets and a broad understanding of the contracts, laws, and tax regulations that apply to real estate transactions. Those first starting out in the industry, without solid connections, may have a hard time establishing themselves and may rely on the help of veteran agents. One way to start building a client base is by offering to hold open houses for other agents, who in return will often agree to pay the rookie agent a portion of the commission earned if a sale results from the open house.

All agents who wish to succeed in the business must have strong communication skills; be willing to generate continual business through cold-calling, networking, and advertising; and put in long hours, often on weekends and evenings. The turnover rate among real estate agents is high, but for those who do succeed, the earning opportunity, depending on the represented market, is unlimited.

JOB OUTLOOK

Unlike much of the rest of the economy, the real estate industry has been doing quite well. Though the robustness varies between sectors, with the residential side of real estate doing best, the industry is hardly in the hangdog state that nearly every other part of the economy seems to be in. However, due to the self-search capability that the Internet offers the public and possibly shifts in the economy, the field of real estate sales will not grow at the same rate as other areas of sales. The BLS reports that job growth will be slower than the average through 2012.

Select your location carefully. And once you're in, be prepared to ride the roller coaster of a cyclical industry. Although the real estate industry is in a protracted boom period right now, veterans assure us that busts will come, and those busts won't be pretty.

Average salaries range from $50,000 to $150,000 or more and can vary according to location, level of effort, luck, and the commission structure between an agent and his or her broker.

On the Job

The Big Picture

Sales Positions

All in a Week's Work

Real People Profiles

The Big Picture

Although different industries offer different sales roles, most of the industries discussed in the previous chapter refer to their salespeople as field representatives or account executives. Sales reps represent the vast majority of career options in sales. And, regardless of title or industry, sales reps typically have three main objectives:

1. Keep existing business

2. Grow existing business

3. Generate new business

Often sales reps also work with their marketing departments to access detailed information about potential clients in order to plan sales strategies. To meet the demands of their prospects and clients, sales reps must be skilled negotiators. Insiders also stress the importance of being able to differentiate their products and services in the eyes of buyers. As one insider puts it, "With so much competition in the field, it's important not to become another commodity. The more we can get the client to see the unique value of our product and its ability to solve their problem, the better chance we have of closing the deal."

Corporate sales also requires managing large accounts that can generate anywhere from $10,000 to millions of dollars in revenue. For those sales reps working on a salary-plus-commission basis, large deals often translate into hefty commissions. Other perks, such as great benefits, a company car, and an expense account for entertaining clients, often come with the job. Of course, not all aspects of the sales process involve personal interaction; sales reps are also expected to generate weekly and monthly sales reports for their managers to record their progress. Attending meetings, conferences, and training sessions, which can often take place at the company's headquarters outside the sales rep's territory, is also mandatory.

Those working in the insurance and real estate industries have a slightly different twist to their roles. Although they may be direct employees of the companies whose products and services they represent, just as traditional sales reps are, many also work for themselves. In both cases, the need to generate new business is constant. These agents work directly with the public, not with other companies. Often their deals aren't on the same large scale as those of sales reps in other industries.

Sales Positions

If you've ever attended a job fair as a college grad, you've probably been introduced to sales jobs in corporate settings where large companies came to recruit bright-eyed, fresh grads into their ranks. It's very likely that independent sales positions such as manufacturer reps and real estate brokers weren't presented as options. As one insider says, "Many people working in sales now had no idea when they first started searching for a job that a career in sales could mean anything other than working for a large company." But the truth is that there are many job options, from private firms to publicly traded companies. You may choose to work in a less stressful environment such as consumer sales or gravitate to the thrill of big deal making in technology.

Generally, there are four sales positions within every industry, each taking on a different title and focus depending on the field, as follows.

MANUFACTURER REPRESENTATIVE

For those working in the manufacturing industry, the title of *manufacturer representative* or *manufacturer's agent* is often applied. Manufacturer representatives are usually independent contractors hired directly by a company to sell its products on the market.

«» **With so much competition in the field, it's important not to become another commodity.**

Reps just starting out in the industry often work as employees of a manufacturing representative firm. Those plastic orange pumpkins and glowing skeletons you buy at the drugstore every Halloween are the specific product of some manufacturing rep. As one insider says, "Think of manufacturing reps as real estate brokers for different industries. They don't take possession of the goods they're selling. They only ensure that the products from the companies that they represent are sold and delivered to the customers (retailers in most cases) that they are calling on."

The fact that most reps are self-employed means that the selling process takes on a double meaning: Not only do manufacturer reps have to sell the products they represent, they must also sell their services to new prospective clients (i.e., manufacturers). This is where a little entrepreneurial know-how can come in handy.

Manufacturer reps usually work on a commission or fee-only basis.

DIRECT CONSUMER SALES

Like manufacturer reps, those involved in direct consumer sales, also known as *business to consumer* or *B2C*, are also titled agents or brokers responsible for working directly with the public on behalf of the seller. They may also be independent contractors or employees. Direct consumer sales reps include insurance and real estate agents and retail sales clerks. These reps meet directly with the public in hopes of selling a product— whether it's a four-bedroom ranch with a mountain view or a life insurance plan or a new set of dishes.

Direct consumer sales positions require impeccable presentation, communication, and social skills over educational experience. These agents must be self-starters as a majority of their earnings are based on a commission structure in which base salaries are minimal. They must also become product experts, understanding any laws that govern the goods they represent. Taking on a direct consumer sales role means spending the bulk of your evening and weekend hours at work, as this is when most customers are available. A real estate broker will spend a significant amount of time outside the office showing properties to potential buyers. Paperwork and follow-up calls are also a major responsibility of direct consumer sales agents, who may spend hours on the computer updating listings or reading about the latest trends in their field.

Due to the growing use of the Internet as a tool for consumer spending, careers in the direct consumer sales business, while available, are less likely to see large growth spurts.

CORPORATE SALES REPRESENTATIVES OR ACCOUNT MANAGERS

When people talk about high-end sales jobs, they're usually referring to positions within corporate sales. This includes a variety of industries from pharmaceuticals and software to financial services. These sales reps work directly with other companies, not the general public, in what is known as *B2B*, or *business-to-business*, sales.

There are many differences between corporate sales and manufacturing or direct consumer sales. People in corporate sales aren't independent contractors; rather, they are direct employees of a single company. It's their job to constantly find new customer prospects, present the company's products and services, close deals, and manage relationships with those accounts.

When recruiting for corporate sales positions, companies usually look for candidates with at least a 4-year degree along with sales experience, preferably in a related field. Having in-depth knowledge or expertise of your field is a must for those corporate sales professionals who often compete against several other companies for the same accounts.

Corporate sales professionals usually bear the job title of *sales representative* or *account manager* and are assigned to large territories, often covering entire regions of the country, to prospect. Territories can also be assigned by specific industry, known as *verticals*, instead of by geographic region. The division of labor according to geography means that travel is a significant part of the corporate sales representative's work—for example, he or she may be required to cover the entire West Coast prospecting new customers.

Corporate sales positions are among the most coveted sales positions because of the higher salary base and more generous commission structure.

SALES MANAGEMENT

Every division within a corporation has its own structure similar to that of the military chain of command. If having direct contact with clients is the equivalent of hunkering down in a foxhole, you may want to aim at a position higher in the organization such as sales manager for a sales territory. Although many of these positions are filled from within by former sales reps, with the right experience and an MBA, you just might be able to start at the management level.

When hiring sales managers, companies look for candidates with at least a 4-year degree, preferably with a master's degree, and a commensurate level of experience in professional sales or business.

The primary role of a sales manager or, as it is often titled, regional sales manager, is to manage the sales representatives within a specific division of the larger sales department— whether it is a specific geographic region or industry. Sales managers are charged with assigning territories, setting goals, providing training, and at times, assisting with larger accounts.

As a sales manager, you can expect longer hours including weekends, increased travel requirements, and more pressure to make sure your region is performing. The perks: less direct sales, a higher base salary, and career advancement toward an executive position.

Competition for sales manager positions is generally greater than for sales rep positions. The BLS reports that the rate of job growth for sales manager positions through 2012 will be faster than the average.

All in a Week's Work

Because day-to-day activities can vary depending on the level of sales activity at any given time, it's easier to get a perspective of a field rep's lifestyle by looking at a traditional weekly schedule.

MONDAY MADNESS

Mondays are usually reserved for meetings and catching up on paperwork, not just for sales but for all industries. That said, sales reps avoid making potentially disruptive calls to customers who are trying to catch up in between all of their meetings. Instead, when they aren't in meetings, reps use the time to follow up on the activities from the previous week. As one insider says, "It's not unusual to have as many as four different meetings on any one Monday. Between strategizing with team members, attending conference calls on product updates, and reporting on the status of your sales cycles, there isn't much time left for getting anything else done."

MIDWEEK FIELD WORK

Tuesdays, Wednesdays, and Thursdays are reserved for hitting the phones and managing the field. This is the time to meet with prospective clients, visit existing accounts, and follow up on new leads. The key to a sales rep's success often lies in the amount of time he or she can get in front of the customer. For pharmaceutical reps, this means visiting doctors' offices to introduce them to new drugs. For consumer reps, it's time to clean up and refurbish product displays, and for tech reps, it's a chance to meet in person with lead contacts for new business.

FRIDAY FORECASTING AND TRACKING

Friday, like Monday, is a time to regroup. Often sales reps need Fridays to catch up on paperwork for the week. Sales managers are constantly asking for updated reports detailing the status of deals and forecast reports—called *pipelines*—that outline a sales rep's goals and sales targets for the next 3 months. These reports are often used as scorecards to measure company success and compiled for use as a tool to report projected earnings to shareholders. Notes must also be made in computerized databases called CRMs, which allow VPs and other execs to view the activity within a sales division. Most companies also adopt some type of sales methodology that includes required paperwork as part of the program.

Real People Profiles

SOFTWARE ACCOUNT EXECUTIVE

Age: 34

Years in field: 3

Education: BA, political science

Work hours per week: 50 or more depending on workload

Size of company: 9,528

Previous experience: hardware and software sales for large companies and start-ups

Annual salary: $80,000 plus commissions

What do you do?

My job title is that of account executive or outside sales rep. My main job is to identify prospective customers, contact them to set up presentations, deliver those presentations, and then manage all sales cycles from start to finish with the goal of closing deals. Along with managing my accounts, I must constantly generate new leads and track the competitors in my assigned territory. I only call on businesses in the life sciences industry; these include pharmaceuticals and medical devices. This is what is known in the sales world as a *vertical* territory instead of those traditionally assigned by geographic regions.

How did you get this job?

When I originally broke into sales, I used a headhunter to help me find a job. After years of working in sales, I then used my technical sales experience and networking skills to obtain this position.

What kind of people do well in this business?

Independent, aggressive, and business-savvy people do the best in technical sales. To be a good rep, you must be able to identify a company's business pains, challenges, and initiatives to successfully leverage your product as a possible technology solution that fits their problem. You must also be able to handle high-stress situations and be able to multitask at all moments. The competition in software sales is really strong, with companies constantly at war to outsell their competitors. Therefore, a lot of stress is put on the reps to close deals.

What is the culture like in your company?

High stress. We are constantly meeting as a team to strategize about our process for bringing in more deals. As a rep, I am responsible for turning in pipeline paperwork that projects my estimated sales for the next 3 months. A good rule of thumb is to always project three times your quota because inevitably two-thirds of your business will drop out. The sales managers then turn in these pipelines along with other paperwork called forecasts, weekly reports on the status of deals, to their boss and so on. The data are used to report back to shareholders. We are always being measured, and this is why there's so much stress in sales to close new deals. Even when you meet your quota, there's no break. You're assigned a larger territory and your next quota is raised. This can definitely result in big commissions, but you have to stay on your toes to keep ahead.

What are the greatest challenges in your work?

Having to sell an ambiguous solution and make it fit a company's requirements especially when you know that a rep from a competitor is just waiting to present next and you have to find a way to make your product more desirable to the customer. Also, keeping up with the paperwork. I spend so much time managing my accounts that I always fall behind with my weekly reports. Companies usually use some type of CRM software. It's a program where you have to log on daily or weekly and jot down notes on the status of your selling cycles. I am always filling mine in last minute.

What are the biggest perks?

One of the reasons I chose to work in software sales is because of the opportunities to make big commissions. My quota is $2 million and if I can meet it, I can make a lot of bonus money. Also, working for a large company comes with extra perks like a fitness membership and even a monthly massage allowance. You can't beat that.

Describe a typical day.

It's hard to describe a typical day because the days vary depending on workload. Most mornings are spent either in meetings with clients or on conference calls with my sales team. When I am not in meetings, I spend part of my day tying up any loose ends associated with a deal such as e-mails or calls to clients, connecting my resource people to an account, and following up on new leads. I then use the rest of my day to hit the phone and make as many new contact calls as I can. Many times even after I have left my office, I spend time at home finishing paperwork.

What is the career track for your profession? How long do people usually stay with one company?

The career track in my industry is to either move up into management or to move on to a more successful company with bigger commission opportunities. People also move from software sales into consulting positions where they can triple their earnings. In software, I would guesstimate that the tenure is pretty short, around 2 years. Companies are always turning over their sales force including management.

What advice would you give to someone looking for a career in sales?

Know how to deal with stress. Also, be smart about the company you choose to work for. There are perks and downsides to every situation. Some people like to work for start-ups, hoping to be a part of something at ground level for bigger payoffs if it takes off. Others like the benefits of working for a big company. Also, learn about the latest trends in an industry. If you can get in as a sales rep selling a product that has a niche market, not only will you feel less like a commodity, you will have more opportunities to make money.

PHARMACEUTICAL SPECIALTY SALES REPRESENTATIVE

Age: 40

Years in business: 10

Education: BS, business administration

Work hours per week: 40

Size of company: 4,037

Previous experience: consumer and pharmaceutical sales

Annual salary: $75,000 plus bonuses

What do you do?

I am a specialty sales rep who promotes prescription and nonprescription drugs to physicians, primarily dermatologists and plastic surgeons.

How did you get your job?

I learned of this opportunity via the newspaper. After making a few contact calls, I landed an interview with one of the regional managers.

What kind of people do well in this business?

People who are highly independent and motivated, and who can be flexible and personable with a variety of people and in a variety of situations. You also need to be able to review clinical data and translate it in a manner that is clear and concise. A person must also be organized and a self-starter to keep up with the ever-changing pace and work that is required.

What is the culture like in your company?

My company is becoming bigger and bigger every day, so there are many protocols and reports that must be followed. Everything is very structured, which is good as long as you're organized and do your work in a timely fashion. In pharmaceutical sales, things are always changing and being updated, so it's a fast-paced setting. The people I work with are very smart, very professional, and very demanding that work be done well and in a timely manner. They are also very helpful, honest, and positive. With any sales job, the bottom line is money, so numbers and market share are always looked at. If you do well, the pressure is not a problem.

What are the greatest challenges in your work?

Maintaining market share and increasing sales. Another is getting the opportunities to make impressions on physicians' prescribing habits. Constantly striving to stay ahead of the reports and paperwork and e-mails is also a challenge. You must also create new ways to sell and new ways to get physicians to continue to prescribe and buy new products. Then getting data 6 to 8 weeks after selling is a long wait—prescription reports don't come out until the information is gathered from pharmacies. With prescription selling, there's no immediate gratification on what you have sold or not sold.

What are the biggest perks?

I'd have to say the independence and flexibility. I am my own manager in many ways and have some flexibility on how I work in my territory. As companies get bigger and start micromanaging more, it does become more difficult. Of course, my manager gives me more freedom and leeway, so a good manager can make or break your job. It's a great job for women with children. Although the work requirements are 8 to 5, there's some flexibility to how you schedule your work and get it done.

Describe a typical day.

Our company requires that you make seven physician calls and two pharmacy calls per day. I cover a large territory due to my specialty and fewer doctors in a geographic location. This means I spend most days on the road. I look at my appointments for the week with doctors as well as prioritize who I need to see and then set my schedule for the day. Our company prioritizes doctors on a list for us, so we put them on a biweekly or monthly call cycle. I usually have objectives for each call and stop in and meet with people who can give me the necessary information or who I need to sell to. When I am not on the road, I am busy completing paperwork, answering e-mails, and making more calls.

What is the career track for your profession?

I am now a national trainer for the Midwest along with being a sales rep. I have also been put on a special task force due to my experience and successes with the company. I may or may not go into management depending on the opportunities. There are a lot of opportunities with pharmaceutical companies, especially for women and minorities looking to get into management positions.

Some new reps will switch jobs from one company to another looking for the right product to sell to the right culture.

What advice would you give to someone looking for a career in sales?

Don't give up on your ideal sales job. With enough perseverance, you will finally get the job you want.

MANUFACTURER REPRESENTATIVE/BUSINESS OWNER

Age: 37

Years in business: 13 (7 years as principal owner)

Education: BS, business administration

Work hours per week: 50

Size of company: 1

Previous experience: consumer sales

Annual compensation: varies, but can exceed $250,000

What are your major responsibilities?

In simple terms, a manufacturer rep sells the products provided for him to people or companies with the ability to buy those products. Companies hire us, in part, because we know the customer's needs and understand how to successfully sell products to that customer. Most important, we know the processes for which our customers purchase those goods. Smaller or start-up companies that wouldn't otherwise be able to obtain appointments are assured that their products are being seen because they are represented by a manufacturer rep.

A true rep places as much importance on the interests of the buyer as he does with the seller. Many of my sales take months to close (and in my industry, they happen on an annual basis), so it's imperative that goods that are presented are a good fit for the buyer's company. Manufacturer reps can sell for as many companies as they can successfully handle.

Where do you work? How do you spend most of your time?

Most of my work is done in the office, although it varies greatly from day to day. Preparation is important and consumes a vast amount of time. And with any sales job, you have to get out of the office to sell. Reps might have to cold-call potential customers, but often they know the majority of the customers within their designated territory. As a rep, you and your company are responsible for knowing the customer's timelines, setting appointments, preparing presentations, presenting products, analyzing the market, preparing quotations, delivering samples, ensuring order deliveries, handling customer service issues, and entertaining customers or manufacturers.

What are some of the pluses?

You're the eyes and ears of the manufacturers you're representing so they depend on you for market information, customer feedback, and account knowledge. Understanding the industry that you're involved in presents endless opportunities. There's also very little monotony. One of the most intriguing parts of the job is the ever-changing opportunities. One day may be filled with selling two lines to customer A, while the next could be presenting four different ones to customer B.

What are the minuses?

Because we aren't tied to one specific product line, representatives are consistently searching for other product lines that might be a good fit for our customers. Finally, as a company owner, I have additional responsibilities that include the everyday tasks of running a business. A manufacturer rep is always dependent on the product that you sell and the customers within your territories. And there are always instances that are out of your control. Companies change location, drop product categories, get bought and sold, and create mediocre items.

How do you get paid?

Manufacturer reps are paid directly by the manufacturer they represent. You'll find that almost all of the compensation agreements are based on a percentage of total dollar sales. Once the product sold is shipped and the manufacturer is paid by the customer, the manufacturer will cut a check to the rep for the previously agreed amount. If no product is sold, there are no commissions earned.

How much travel is involved?

Typically, the travel is within the representative's designated territory. However, many retailers often send their buyers on trips to manufacturing facilities or trade shows, both domestically and internationally. If the companies that we represent have offices, showrooms, or booth space in the areas that the retailers are visiting, the manufacturer rep will accompany them throughout the trip.

How is this type of position different from those in other industries?

You're an independent contractor, and compensation is based solely on performance. There typically aren't the office politics that occur in a corporate environment, and there is an unlimited amount of opportunities.

How do beginners break into the field?

Most manufacturers want to have people who are familiar with the industry, or at least the customers that they're targeting, when hiring a rep. You can gain experience by working for retailers in a specific industry or manufacturers that make goods for that industry. Firms also want someone with sales experience. Still, there are manufacturer rep companies that will hire somebody directly out of college. If you join a reputable firm, you'll be given the tools and the direction necessary to begin. With success, promotions will come in the form of being assigned to sell to larger customers within the firm's territory.

BUSINESS DEVELOPMENT SALES

Age: 31

Years in business: 9

Education: BA, philosophy

Work hours per week: 45

Size of company: 65

Previous experience: operations, sales, business, and product development

Annual salary: $100,000 not including bonuses

What do you do?

Business development for an Internet marketing company. What I do day to day is make contacts at targeted companies, create relationships, and try to sign distribution deals for our products.

How did you get this career?

I didn't really look for it; I just sort of fell into the sales role. Coming out of college I took the first job offered to me, and it happened to be in door-to-door copier sales. I absolutely hated it. The thought of heading out to an office complex every day to sell a product to people who may or (more likely) may not need it was a terrible proposition. I left there to go to an Internet start-up and quickly moved into sales there, again just falling into the role.

How could someone get a job like yours?

My current job I would consider a second- or third-tier sales job. By this I mean you have to have sales experience to get my current job. A first-tier sales job is generally one that is inside sales, without face-to-face client meetings, and typically you're micromanaged—down to how many calls you make and prospects you find every day.

The job I am in now is not that job. Your bosses expect you to perform and bring in accounts but they also expect that you know how to make calls and how to engage clients without having to monitor your progress daily. Overall, to get a job like this, you need to start off in the trenches, selling long distance or inside sales at a reputable company.

What kind of people do well in your business?

There are two types: (1) People who are methodical. These people are the ones who are banging out 50 calls a day and are often trying the same person twice a day. (2) Trustworthy, diligent people. These are the types of people who are inherently trusted in everyday life. They go into a meeting and create a level of trust right off the bat.

What is the culture like in your company?

Entrepreneurial, supportive, relaxed, but professional.

What are the greatest challenges in your work?

Keeping a high level of motivation. The job can be draining. You're only as good as your last sale. There are constant expectations.

What are the biggest perks?

The money, autonomy, and the rush of making a sale.

What is the career track for your profession? How long do people usually stay with one company?

There's not much of a career track unless you want to get into sales management, and most good salespeople don't. They don't want to get into management because generally you make more money being a salesperson.

People generally don't stay with one company too long either. As I said before, you're only as good as your last sale, and if you do really well, the expectations are that you will always perform. When you've had a bad couple of months or year, you get sick of not making as much money and the company wants someone in who is hungry, so you generally move on. It's also high pressure and so the average life in the same sales job is about 2 to 3 years, I would bet.

What advice would you give to someone looking for a career in sales?

Pick a product you believe in. You can't sell something that doesn't work, or at least that you don't believe works. Also, make sure you're working with good, smart people who will support you.

The Workplace

Culture

Job Stress

Workplace Diversity

Travel

Compensation

Vacation

Perks

Career Path

Insider Scoop

Culture

There's something about sales that evokes the promise of high pressure, fast talk, and the exchange of large amounts of money that careers in library science or environmental studies fail to evoke. The field of sales is one filled with unbridled energy where the opportunity to succeed is as great as the opportunity to fail. If you prefer talking to your cat to small talk with acquaintances, sales is probably not the career for you. But if you're ready to interact with complete strangers and spend countless hours promoting the value of a product or service with the potential for a big payoff, then a sales career may be just what you're looking for.

ORGANIZATIONAL FACTORS

Sales is integral to all types of businesses, big and small, and as such, you'll find that the culture can vary greatly from one company to another. Is the company you're looking at one that employs hundreds or thousands of people, or is it a small firm with a more intimate setting? Has the company gone public and thus obligated to report to its shareholders, or is it privately held with more room for flexibility? Is the sales staff exclusively in-house, or do reps work in the field as well? All of these factors influence the culture that shapes a sales rep's lifestyle.

It's worth noting, however, that within any number of industries you can find exceptions to these rules.

Public vs Private

In general, the culture within a public company can often be much more structured, numbers-driven, and process-oriented than that of a private firm. Public companies must provide accurate reporting of their sales numbers to shareholders on a continual basis. This translates into a trickle-down effect in which stress is placed on sales reps to produce strong numbers. The recent criticism big companies have received for overstating their numbers have put added stress on top sales execs to deliver.

In contrast, private companies that don't have to answer to shareholders tend to adopt a more laid-back work culture. Many times these companies have casual dress codes and refrain from micromanaging the activities of their sales reps.

Management

In the end, it's the style of the executive team that will drive the culture of a company. Those with more conservative views, whether the company is big or small, will push for stricter standards when it comes to company procedures and policies, whereas companies started by more out-of-the-box thinkers, such as those computer geniuses who got their start working out of their garages, will be more likely to encourage employee individualism.

In(side) or Out(side)?

Consider too that in large companies the sales division is made up of both an inside and outside sales force. However, a smaller company may depend solely on an inside sales staff or outside field reps to generate business. Depending on how it's set up, a company can exhibit a strong culture or none at all. Inside sales departments are structured much differently than regional offices for field reps. Inside sales reps work specifically in an office setting and seldom, if ever, meet face-to-face with their clients. They usually work on smaller deals through phone and e-mail contact, answer requests for more product information, and generate leads for outside field reps. Often they are telemarketers required to reach a quota of calls each day. Working alongside other sales reps often creates a feeling of camaraderie. Shared pressures, job responsibilities, and sales goals help create bonds that outside reps often say is lacking in a field sales operation.

Outside field reps who spend much of their time telecommuting or on the road may also lack any sense of company culture in their work. However, many sales reps also spend an average of 3 days a week in a regional or satellite office with others on their sales team. These include other field reps, their sales manager, resource people, and those handling legal contracts.

The Stress Test

The culture is often measured on a high-stress to high-risk to high-reward ratio—meaning that the more stress reps feel and the more risk there is in failing to generate new business, the more rewards there are for closing big deals. Often, reps accustomed to making big numbers are also accustomed to expensive lifestyles. This often becomes the strongest motivator for successful performance. A "go big or go home" attitude prevails across the sales world and often fuels the intensity in sales offices.

TRENDS AFFECTING CULTURE

The Not-So-New Economy

The biggest factor at work in the field of sales as a whole is the less-than-stellar economy of the last 5 years, which required many companies to lay off employees. This means that remaining staff is being stretched, forced to do more with fewer resources and less support. Time has become a precious resource and has made the workplace much more stressful and competitive. How have these staff reductions affected sales reps? In addition to leaving existing sales reps with larger territories, these layoffs often occur at client companies, resulting in a sales audience that is just as overworked and often operating with much smaller budgets. The increasing demands on clients' time often mean sales reps have little, if any, time to make the sale.

In the past, a round of golf and a good dinner were often all it took to secure a deal. But now with little time available for afternoon retreats, reps are forced to find creative ways to get the attention of potential clients. This has led to more companies investing in research into the psychology of sales, including the psychology of sales language and the emotions behind buying decisions. In many instances, a client's decision to buy is not a rational action and involves more complex interactions with a sales rep. By capitalizing on the psychology behind spending trends, companies are better preparing their sales staffs to perform under time-crunched conditions.

Technology

Technological advances have also forced huge shifts in the relationship between sellers and buyers. First and foremost, access to the Internet has led to more informed buyers. Now buyers have access to all baseline data across the board, making the competition to win them over even more complex. On the other hand, technological advances have also alleviated one of the biggest challenges for sales reps in the past—around establishing contact with potential leads. With the use of e-mail, cell phones, instant messaging, and voice mail, making contact is now much easier. What has become more crucial is how those 30 seconds of client contact are used. These days, reps are able to work more independently from the field. A large percent of field reps telecommute from home when not traveling to meet with clients.

Focus on Human Capital

Another buzz in the work culture of many companies is the idea of maximizing human capital. No longer can employees such as sales reps be viewed as another replaceable cog in the wheel. With the cost of turnover so high, many companies have taken a more holistic approach to managing their workforce. Many companies today are making efforts to improve work/life balance for employees by offering resources and support previously not considered an employer's responsibility, such as on-site child care, free financial planning services, or flexibility around work schedules and family emergencies. Although sales reps often complain that they are the last ones to be given any room to breathe, a definite shift in attitudes and cultures is taking place in many organizations.

Job Stress

Imagine you're in the car on your way to your fourth appointment of the day, after already spending the morning in meetings with various prospective clients while playing phone tag with a contact for a deal you've been working on for months. As you turn into the parking lot for your next appointment, you receive a call from a new customer requesting a specific piece of information on a deal you just closed. With only 10 minutes to spare, you immediately instant message another rep in the office with access to a computer for assistance retrieving the data. Just when you think you have tied up all of your loose ends, your manager calls to get an update on your activities for the day. This is a common scenario in the sales world, where reps must juggle multiple tasks on an hourly basis to keep up with an increasingly competitive field. The result: a high level of job stress.

What is the cause of so much stress? Businesses rely heavily on their sales forces to meet extremely aggressive goals. Sales numbers are also the most tangible measure available to companies wishing to gauge the employee performance. Numbers drive quarterly goals. And as sales reps become more successful, the expected quota keeps rising, leaving many feeling as if their efforts will never be good enough. Some love the chase and the challenge, while others find the endless and often escalating pressure overwhelming. As one insider says, "There's always an end. You must meet your numbers by the end of the month, end of the quarter, end of the year. Time can begin to feel like your enemy."

Another factor that can contribute to job stress is the lack of structure underlying a sales rep's daily work. The nature of the work is sporadic, resulting in uneven workloads, with intensely busy periods followed by stretches of relative inactivity. Calls with existing clients are usually less stressful than new client contacts. And, the larger the deal, the greater the number of people involved. With so many fingers in the pie, a rep is faced with managing a multitude of variables and personalities that could go haywire at any moment.

The leadership provided within a sales division can help make the day-to-day stress more manageable. However, in the end, sales reps will always be under constant pressure to meet new clients, find fresh opportunities, and close big deals. With so much at stake for a business predicated on hitting aggressive sales numbers, stress is part and parcel of the job.

Workplace Diversity

Over the last few decades, diversity in the workplace has become a significant issue for employers. Many companies are looking to strengthen their workforce through recruiting practices that target minorities. They recognize that a more diverse workforce—across all levels—is better able to serve a diverse audience. Although the field of sales is still dominated by white males, there is growth in all forms of diversity within its ranks, especially when it comes to opportunities for women and minorities. Sales is performance-driven, and as such opportunities are available for anyone willing to put in the time and effort to hit these performance goals. The bottom line is whether you can produce, build relationships, and manage your own schedule.

Corporations such as Eli Lilly have implemented strategies to promote diversity across their workforce. The African American Network, Lilly Deaf Network, and Women's Network are just a few of the many support groups dedicated to the practice of inclusive work environments, networking opportunities for employees with shared interests and culture, and awareness-building within the entire workforce on diversity issues. Development and advancement of female employees has become a centerpiece of career development practices at other large companies as well. Procter & Gamble reports that the number of women and minorities at the vice president and manager levels has doubled over the past 5 years. Eli Lilly and Procter & Gamble were both named to *Working Mother*'s 2004 list of the "100 Best Companies for Working Mothers."

To find out more about a company's diversity practices, check its website to see whether it has section on diversity. You can also look at the lists and rankings of companies offering the best opportunities to minorities, such as those from *Working Mother, Fortune*, and *DiversityInc*. If the company you're considering is small, it likely won't make the top 100 lists, as they usually have specific size requirements for inclusion. In that case, talk to alum who work at these companies to get the skinny on whether diversity is a key concern for management at these firms. You can also ask about diversity initiatives at the company in your interviews.

Travel

Most sales reps, if asked, will agree that the lyrics from "On the Road Again" pretty much sum it up. But the amount of time spent on the road and the distance covered depends on the industry, account sizes, and assigned territory. Some sales professionals such as real estate agents focus on particular neighborhoods whereas manufacturer reps may be assigned to entire regions of the country.

Sales reps in insurance, real estate, and certain consumer product sectors will find that travel requirements are confined to local areas. The target market for these sales reps is usually in the communities where they live; the familiarity of their name in association with their occupation in a specific city or town plays a key part in their networking practice. Because these reps work directly with consumers, becoming active members of local organizations such as the Chamber of Commerce or Toastmasters Club is more important than trying to prospect clients statewide. Although not required to travel great distances, these reps, especially in areas such as real estate, do spend a great deal of time in their cars driving to client meetings. This is also true many sales reps in consumer goods who are assigned to specific vendors, such as drugstores, in an assigned territory of a state. After all, these reps are expected to manage store displays, refurbish and rotate products, and maintain a sound customer base.

Pharmaceutical reps, although assigned to cover a much larger territory within a state, usually focus on a specific region that includes numerous physicians and hospitals. Some companies will even provide a company car and an expense account for travel costs and client meals. Depending on the quota, pharmaceutical reps usually put in a minimum of 3 days on the road visiting clients. Although part of a sales rep's job is to generate new leads, reps also call on the same doctors time and again—a key reason many insiders consider pharmaceutical sales less stressful than sales positions in other industries. As one insider says, "I have 250 doctors on my client call list, but my company has targeted that around 100 of those actually write the most prescriptions using our product. This means that 80 percent of my business comes from those targeted doctors."

Sales reps who manage larger accounts will likely travel all around the country to close large deals in which the final decision requires a presentation to executives at company headquarters. Those in corporate or B2B relationships are assigned large territories that cover several states. A territory covered by one company rep could be as big as the entire West Coast. It's also not unusual for a sales rep handling large accounts to call on clients in several different cities in a given month.

Whether they're in the pharmaceutical or tech industry, sales reps are frequently required to travel to product and sales training meetings as well. Training usually begins with a kickoff party at the beginning of the year. It typically lasts a week and is filled with parties, lectures, training sessions, and meetings. Often the kickoff will be held at corporate headquarters, but some companies may opt for hot spots like Las Vegas. Additional training will take place all across the country on an ongoing schedule for the rest of the year. In most cases, training seminars are mandatory, but some training courses are optional and intended for reps seeking more support. Most training sessions, though paid for by the company, involve some weekend and evening events, travel, or both.

Compensation

Although there are many factors to consider when weighing specific job offers or target industries, most sales professionals assign the greatest importance to the quality of the compensation packages being compared. Compensation is more than just the paycheck brought home at the end of the week. Compensation includes the entire set of monetary rewards—from base salary, to signing and performance bonuses, to commissions, to incentive awards—and the comparative value of the benefits package, which range from the traditional—such as retirement planning and health coverage—to the unconventional—such as voluntary pet insurance. These packages vary based on company size and style of operations.

BASE SALARY

Every job profile has one common denominator: the amount offered as the base salary. The salary for a sales rep position is based on job requirements, competitors' salary base for the same position, the strength of the marketplace, and the candidate's level of experience. Each industry has its own salary range and structure. Those with larger account responsibilities usually offer bigger base salaries, whereas many B2C companies use commission incentives to compensate for lower base salaries. And never underestimate the power of negotiation, especially when demand for professional sales reps is high. Although newcomers to the field lack negotiating leverage, for those with more experience and expertise, the base salary presented in the initial offer is typically just a starting point.

COMMISSIONS AND BONUSES

One aspect of sales that sets it apart from many other careers is the opportunity to earn extra money in the form of commissions and performance bonuses. Along with a base salary, many sales jobs include the opportunity to earn money in excess of regular sells. For pharmaceutical and consumer reps, this usually comes in the form of a bonus given after a rep meets his or her yearly quota. Reps who work in this soft sales industry (where sells are done indirectly) receive bonuses instead of commissions, unless they also represent a product that they sell directly to the customer. In other industries such as technology, sales reps have the opportunity to earn commissions on each deal they close or after closing a percentage of their quota. Commission sales positions usually involve more stress than those only offering bonuses. Likewise, commission-only positions (i.e., those with no base salary) place ultimate responsibility on the reps. For example, in the real estate industry, many agents make their entire earnings from commissions on sales. In most cases, this hovers in the area of 6 percent and is often split between the rep and his or her supervising broker.

When looking for a sales position, beware of those jobs offering commission-only compensation. This is usually sales lingo for "you earn what you sell." Commission-only positions force the rep to bear the brunt of market conditions and product issues that influence sales but are outside the reps' control, such as an economic downturn or faulty manufacturing.

BENEFITS

Given the rising cost of health care, a generous insurance package is no longer icing on the cake but the flour holding it together. One plus of working for most large companies is the great coverage a group plan offers. If you've ever worked as an independent contractor, you know how expensive purchasing individual insurance can be, only to receive partial coverage with high deductibles. Almost all companies offer their employees basic health care coverage, which usually includes coverage for an employee's immediate family and in some situations for domestic partners. Most companies offer their employees a choice among several health plans, including PPO or HMO plans, in addition to prescription drug, dental, and vision coverage, though some companies don't offer all of these. Some employers also offer disability and life insurance options.

Most companies also offer full-time employees retirement planning options, such as a 401(k), with or without matching employer contributions, or a pension plan. All companies will offer a standard maternity leave package, which usually translates into 6 weeks of paid leave with the option for additional unpaid time when requested.

Vacation

Taking time off from a job that never slows down enough to let you jump off the merry-go-round may feel like an impossible dream. In fact, at some companies, taking time off at the end of a fiscal year or quarter could be grounds for termination. But for those who put in long hours chasing deals, a little rest and relaxation may be exactly what's needed to recharge the proverbial battery. Vacation and paid-time-off programs will vary depending on the industry and company. Some companies set specific time-off structures based on position and time employed. A standard example is 2 weeks' paid vacation for the first year of work, with vacation time increasing with each year of employment. Other sales reps may accumulate days off based on hours earned for the amount of time in service. For example, after a month of work, a rep may receive 8 to10 hours of banked time. These hours add up over a year, turning into days which can be taken all at once or in smaller lump amounts for daily or weekend retreats.

After a specific length of time with a company, such as 5 or 10 years, some companies offer additional days of recognized vacation time. Along with vacation time, paid days are often provided for sick or personal leave, including absence due to illness or death in the family. Again, some companies have a very complex structure for their personal leave plans, which allots specific amounts of time off depending on the cause. Others give a set amount of personal leave time at the beginning of an employment year to be used at the discretion of the employee and with the approval of the supervising manager. To keep people in the field, some companies also offer monetary incentives in return for unused vacation or personal leave time or roll unused time into the next year. Meanwhile, other companies have a "use it or lose it" policy, which limits the total number of vacation or paid-time-off days that can be accrued, so that any days over the limit are lost.

Perks

If the accessories make the outfit, the perks a company offers can set it apart from its competitors. With the need to recruit and retain a strong workforce, companies are getting more creative with the incentives they offer. What kind of perks can you expect as a sales rep? Don't assume that larger companies will offer the best perks. Although these companies may have more money, size doesn't always drive a creative approach to rewarding employees. In fact, being able to offer unique incentives has become an important way for companies who cannot afford higher base salaries to compete with others in their industry that can.

One perk to look for that benefits both employer and employee is an education reimbursement and/or leave package. These packages not only offer time away from the field for further educational training, but also reimburse employees through company funds. Bear in mind that firms that do offer reimbursement may do so under the condition that the employee remain an employee for a designated length of time after the education has been completed.

Many companies offer free financial planning services, flexible spending accounts, reimbursement for commuting expenses, and charitable gift programs where the company matches donations made by an employee to a charitable organization of choice.

Perks can also come in the form of personal incentives. These include allowances for fitness memberships, day-care centers, and adoption assistance programs. If you're a strong performer, you could win awards such as Sales Rep of the Year that include a cash prize or paid vacation to a five-star resort, for example.

Career Path

In general, the best place to find advancement opportunities is within one company. Who better to fill an open position than someone who already understands company procedures and policies, who has good working relationships with others at the company, and who has already earned the respect and confidence of peers and managers? The natural progression of moving up within the ranks may start with members of an inside sales team who spend years generating leads for outside reps to prospect, and who in turn become field reps themselves.

Many field reps with proven track records in their territories are then assigned larger territories or accounts. If they continue to perform strongly, they are often asked to take on one of two roles. The first might be a corporate role such as that of a sales trainer developing new talent for the field. The second entails taking on a managerial role, managing the selling cycles of an assigned group of reps, and less, if any, direct selling. However, many reps aren't interested in becoming managers as this often means forgoing the flexibility that the field offers. In addition, becoming a manager does not necessarily mean increased compensation. Some of the top reps in the field can earn more than their managers. Unwanted pressure to advance into a managerial role can present a dilemma for sales reps worried about the repercussions of turning down such advancement opportunities.

Depending on the size of the organization, a sales manager looking to advance to the next rung can set his or her sights on becoming the vice president of a sales division within a company. The sales VP supervises the sales managers and usually reports directly to the CEO.

As with nearly all promotions, there are associated increases in pay and responsibilities. Candidates who want to advance must consider all of the pros and cons that will accompany a change in position. Will it mean relocating to corporate headquarters? Will work hours increase along with the stress? Will it help you achieve your professional goals?

You can also advance your career by changing companies. Larger companies often offer greater base salaries and bigger commissions. A sales rep may choose to move to another company in the same industry, where her experience gives her more negotiating power. But for a rep who has earned a reputation as an aggressive seller with experience in fiercely competitive markets such as technical sales, a wider range of career options across industries often becomes available.

If you're working in an independent sales position, such as real estate agent or manufacturer rep, the next step is typically to go into business for yourself and become your own boss. This path brings more responsibilities as well as increased earning potential.

Insider Scoop

WHAT INSIDERS LOVE

Ka-Ching!

One of the most appealing aspects of working in sales is the potential for huge earnings. With many companies offering competitive base salaries and bonus opportunities, sales has become a hot job for those with the ability to bring in the deals. The financial rewards available vary from industry to industry, with those requiring the management of large accounts—such as software sales—offering larger payoffs than indirect sales industries such as pharmaceuticals. As one insider says, "I chose to work in the high-tech sales arena because of the six-figure earning potential that comes from closing big sales with large corporations. A commission on a single deal can range anywhere from $5,000 to $200,000 dollars."

Flex Time

Flex time is one of the hottest topics circling Corporate America these days. And while people working in management and human resources may find a flexible schedule impossible to maintain, a flexible schedule is often just what's needed to thrive in sales: Some days may require a sales rep to put in 12 hours on the road, whereas others leave time for personal appointments and paperwork. This is one reason the sales profession is so popular with women. As one insider says, "Working in sales as a mother of four allows for the occasional interruption in the work day to attend a school play or take my child to a dentist appointment."

Hail the Smorgasbord

Another aspect of sales that those in the profession love is the multitude of opportunities a sales career can offer. It is not uncommon for those working in sales to change jobs every couple of years to find a fresh arena in which to compete. Sales is a part of every flourishing business, so if your interest lies in athletics, you can pursue a career with sporting manufacturers. For those who love technology, there are lucrative opportunities at high-tech companies such as Microsoft.

Feeling Perky?

Whether it's a company car or entertaining clients while attending a Major League Baseball game, the perks associated with sales have reps smiling. One insider says, "It's especially fun if you're single because there are so many functions to attend and people to meet." Employees of larger corporations may receive perks such as adoption assistance and free fitness club memberships. And sales professionals usually receive handsome discounts on the products they sell.

The Triple X Effect

Like the adrenaline racing through the veins of an extreme athlete flying in the air on his motorcross bike over a crowd of cheering fans, sales professionals say the fast-paced world of sales—although at times taxing—fuels their love of the job. As one insider says, "The thrill

" A commission on a single deal can range anywhere from $5,000 to $200,000 dollars.

is often in the accomplishment of closing a deal. Sometimes the actual rush that comes from the win becomes even greater than the financial rewards." If you want to work in a challenging, high-risk environment with high potential returns, then sales is a perfect match. It's the chase of the sale that keeps many professionals in the field, fueled by the unpredictable nature of the industry.

WATCH OUT!

The Commodity Factor

The increasing competition associated with selling products and services today, coupled with an even more sophisticated marketplace, often leaves sales professionals feeling like a commodity. The days when all it took was representing the right hot product from an aspiring new company to ensure that clients were as eager as reps to set up a meeting to close a deal are over for most sales professionals. With more and more products to choose from on the market, many reps complain of feeling like another number in a long line of competitors, hoping to say the right words to grab a client's interest. Sales cycles for single accounts often take longer to close than in the past and are shaky up to the last second. As one insider says, "A deal can change in a second and until you have it in writing, you can't count on anything."

Surviving the Pressure Cooker

There are always new numbers to meet when you work in sales as companies continually try to boost profits and keep investors happy. The pressure to produce most often falls on the shoulders of those in the sales department. As managers track the performance of their reps, sales professionals complain that the constant threat of losing their job is always hovering. No matter how strong the last quarter was, employers are constantly pressuring their sales staff to outperform past numbers. This often leads to high levels of job stress and a blistering burnout rate among those in the profession.

Losing Your Steam

Another challenge for those working in sales is the need to be a self-starter. As one insider says, "Keeping your motivation high in order to attract new clients is a constant struggle." But because the need to bring in new business never eases and most sales reps find themselves alone in the field without daily contact with their working peers, being your own cheerleader takes real ingenuity. This is why many sales professionals turn to private coaches to help inspire and revive their selling techniques. Finding a product that you believe in is another way to avoid quick burnout on the job. The importance of loving what you do can make all the difference when motivation to sell begins to wane.

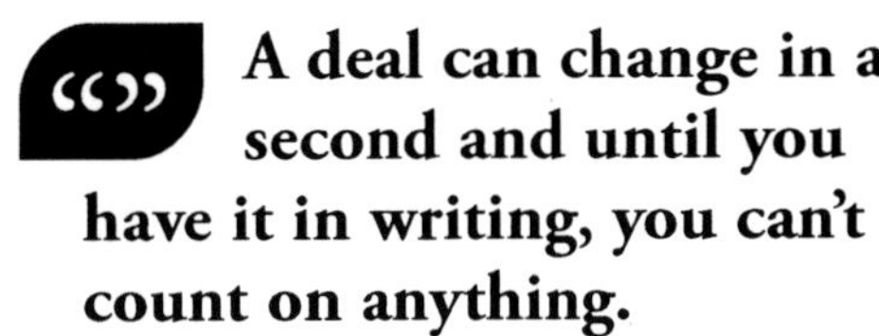

A deal can change in a second and until you have it in writing, you can't count on anything.

Missing Persons Report

Long hours on the road and erratic schedules often leave those working in sales feeling like candidates for the back of a milk carton. Top sales reps are often those willing to put in endless hours hitting the phones, visiting with prospective clients, and criss-crossing country to close deals. As one insider says, "Your job becomes your life, leaving only a few precious moments on the weekend to reconnect with family and run errands." Sales reps also complain that employers are more concerned with meeting numbers than the well-being of their reps, expecting sales members to put in the hours or find a new job.

Getting Hired

The Recruiting Process

Skills and Education

Preparing for the Interview

Interviewing Tips

Getting Grilled

Grilling Your Interviewer

The Recruiting Process

With the recent economic downturn and resulting wave of downsizing finally coming to a halt, companies are eager to find ways to increase profits. The surest way is with a strong sales force. In fact, *Fortune* magazine recently reported that of 65 North American companies, 77 percent are recruiting new sales reps and 50 percent are looking to add telephone and Web-based salespeople to their divisions. With the added factor of high job turnover, companies are hard pressed to recruit, train, and keep good reps.

Impeccable presentation skills are the name of the game when interviewing for a sales position. Remember, sales reps are the face of the company. Employers want people who are confident, well spoken, and intelligent to represent their company and its products and services. But don't get confuse intelligence with arrogance. Any personal qualities or habits that are likely to put off clients won't sit well with sales hiring managers either. Do your research ahead of time. Know the company's key people, product or service details, and the latest trends in the industry. Salespeople must be experts in the field, so your preparation for interviews will go a long way toward convincing prospective employers that you will approach the sales process, which is really another sort of interview, with the same thorough preparation.

UNDERGRADUATES

Campus resources are an excellent way to begin the job hunt. Companies often build strong relationships with colleges in hopes of recruiting new employees. Remember, not only are you looking for a job, but companies are also looking for you. College career centers will post upcoming job fairs and recruiting opportunities on a continual basis. Often, you can sign up to receive e-mail announcements of upcoming recruiting events. Once you've taken a look at the list of visiting companies, do your research. Target those companies of the most interest to you and study, study, study. Who is the VP of sales? What are the company's product specifications?

You can also apply to targeted companies using online forms on their websites (if available) or by contacting the human resources departments. Most companies have a career section on their site with current job postings, specific job descriptions, and detailed steps for application. This will also give you a chance to learn more about your prospective employer. Networking with friends and family is also a great way to find job leads. Don't be shy about making contact with those already working in the field. Not only will they offer the inside scoop on the field, they may also be able to connect you with job opportunities.

MBAS

Although most sales managers come up through the ranks of a company, employers also turn to MBAs when looking to fill higher-level positions. Along with your degree, however, experience in the industry will be a huge plus. MBAs are often brought onto a team to help with overall sales strategy and marketing. Your best opportunities are in sales consulting. Executive positions within a company are also typically reserved for those who've attained higher-education degrees. This does not mean that you can expect to land a job as VP of sales at a large firm right out of business school. However, having a degree will set you on the right path.

Job fairs specifically aimed at recruiting MBAs take place on a regular basis on most campuses. These provide a great opportunity for MBA students to meet one-on-one with potential employers. MBAs should also take advantage of all networking resources. These include professional organizations, university alumni events, and contacts already working in the field. Going online to monitor opportunities on job boards or specific company websites is another way to generate leads. The more active you are in the search, the more possibilities you can drum up. To save time, focus your search on industries that match your long-term career plan. MBAs looking to move up the ranks should view job opportunities with a strategic agenda in mind.

MIDCAREER CANDIDATES

Sales experience and an already established network of contacts make midcareer candidates prime targets for corporate recruiters. It's not uncommon for companies to contact their competitors' tops sales executives with job offers. But don't wait for your phone to ring. Taking advantage of the network you've built over years of business dealings could be the key to a new job. It's also important to check job boards, attend job fairs, and individual company websites when hunting.

You may also find career advancement opportunities within your own company. Check out all of your options before making a big change. Becoming a specialty rep, senior executive with a larger territory, sales trainer, or moving into management may be the best career move for you. Changing companies or industries could result in more job stress. Consider that you would be working within a different culture, learning a new product, and building a client base from the ground level. Sales reps with experience in only one industry may also find it hard to move into another sector of sales. But for those with experience in what is considered hard sales, the reputation for being an aggressive salesperson often affords you instant credibility.

Skills and Education

Because sales positions and responsibilities vary with the industries they serve, desired skills and educational backgrounds will also vary by company and industry. The more complex a company's business is, the more education required. However, those wishing to go into real estate or insurance may find that an associate's degree is enough to land a job. When recruiting new sales reps, whether for inside or field positions, most companies require candidates to have at least a 4-year degree. But because experience in sales tends to outweigh educational background, companies aren't as picky about the type of degree. Larger companies tend to look for new hires with degrees relevant to their industry. A banking company, for example, looks for candidates with finance backgrounds, whereas a medical sales recruiter seeks biology majors. Popular degrees among all companies hiring reps, whether in real estate management or field sales, are those in the areas of business administration, sales, and marketing.

What's most important to companies hiring new sales reps is the degree of sales experience a candidate possesses. For those breaking into the industry, even a summer job selling posters is evidence that you have some understanding of the basic elements in sales. Non-entry-level sales positions often require a minimum of 3 to 5 years of experience in a related field.

Of course, what you lack in experience can be made up in character. Most sales job postings describe ideal candidates as having strong presentation, organization, time-management, written, verbal, and problem-solving skills. They must be market-savvy, innovative, and knowledgeable. Management and executive positions usually require even more education and experience, and although many managers rise up through the ranks from entry-level sales rep positions, those hired from outside the company are usually required to have an MBA.

Preparing for the Interview

As with so many other things, the key to acing a job interview is in your preparation:

1. Know your career aspirations. Be prepared to talk about why working in sales interests you. Frame your professional and academic background in relation to the position you hope to acquire. Make sure to emphasize any sales experience no matter how small. Also, be sure to present yourself as someone who is knowledgeable about the current trends in the industry. Keeping updated on the latest trends in product and service development is a must for those working in sales.

2. Do your research. We can't stress this enough. Uninformed applicants are an immediate turnoff. As a sales rep, you will be required to know complex information about your product or service and able to discuss it with ease. Research the company and product or service you will be selling if you get the job. Though a large part of the interview will be about you, it's important to show that you already having a working knowledge of the company and product. Not only does this convey real interest, it establishes that you're aware of how important it is to become an expert on product information in sales. You should also know the corporate structure, any parent or subsidiary companies, who the executives are, how the company has been doing in its niche market, and more.

3. Be prepared to explain why you want to work for this company as opposed to others. "I hear you guys are really awesome to work for" doesn't cut it. What is it about the company's product or service that interests you? Why are your skills and background a good fit with the company? People who want to get hired for high level sales and management positions are expected to say that they have experience calling on C-level contacts, meaning CEOs and CFOs. Include all prior sales experience since it's what employers are looking for. Tip: Other bad answers include those having to do with location, salary, and hours (e.g., "How many hours will I have to work?")

Interviewing Tips

If there was ever a time to let your selling abilities shine, it's in the interview. Like it or not, an interview is an audition and you're up for the part against numerous other applicants. Those qualities and experiences that set you apart are what could land you the job. Sales interviews differ from other types of job interviews in that the qualities you present in the interview are the same qualities you will use in the field. It should come as no surprise then that your presentation skills and depth of knowledge will be heavily weighted factors. Fortunately, you can, and should, use this fact to your advantage.

Once a company has received your resume, they will set up your initial interview. This may be done in person or over the phone. And although phone interviews aren't the ideal way to meet future employers, it's a reality of the recruiting process. Find a comfortable chair, keep a copy of your resume and cover letter in front of you for reference, and pretend you're in the room with the interviewer. Answer questions as clearly and concisely as possible.

For those lacking sales experience or high GPAs, the face-to-face interview is a great chance to show off your skill set. Here are some tips for putting your best foot forward:

- Dress professionally. Image is very important in sales. If you get the job, you will be representing the company in the field.

- Bring several copies of your resume with you. Include all sales experience, especially internship and jobs in related fields. Let your resume speak for you and enjoy the process.

- Arrive promptly and well rested.

- Use good listening skills. With the shift in companies toward more consultative, relational selling processes, today's sales reps need to be good listeners as well as communicators.

- Although most of the interview will be focused on you, asking good questions is the key to understanding the job. Ask questions that will clarify your understanding of the job, department goals, and direction of the company. Recruiters consider it a sign of true interest.

- Ask about specifics involved in the hiring process, what next steps might be, and so on.

Getting Grilled

Take a deep breath. Although no one can predict exactly what an interviewer will ask, most questions will revolve around your educational background, sales experience, and interest in the position.

Following are examples of the types of questions you can expect to be asked—and should be prepared to answer—in the interview. You can also expect a few pointed questions designed to test your broad knowledge of the company's industry and your specific knowledge of the company's products and services.

- Why do you want to work for us?

- What do you know about our company?

- Why did you choose your college major?

- What previous sales experience do you have?

- Do you have experience calling on C-level contacts (i.e., CEOs, CFOs.)?

- What were your responsibilities at your previous position?

- Why did you leave your previous job?

- Tell me about a mistake you've made and what you learned from it.

- What type of work environment do you like?

- What qualities do you look for in a manager?

- How do you handle stress?

- Where do you expect to be in 5 years? In 10?

- What skills would you bring to our company?

- What accomplishment are you most proud of?

- Describe a situation where your sales expertise proved effective.

- What was the last book you read?

- What skills would you most like to improve?

- What are your greatest strengths? Weaknesses?

Grilling Your Interviewer

Now it's your turn. Every interview is a conversation, and you'll be expected to ask a few questions of your own. This is your best opportunity not only to learn more specific job details but to hear about the company's overall culture as well. We've listed some good general questions here and categorized them by their level of aggression. Those in the "Rare" section are softball questions, while the "Well Done" questions will put the fire under your interviewer's feet. Not all of the questions may be appropriate to your situation, so plan ahead. Be sure to arrive at an interview prepared with questions specific to the company.

RARE

- What size is the territory I would be covering?

- How large is the team I'd be working with? How do team members communicate?

- What is the selling methodology used by this company?

- Is training provided? If so, what kind?

- What are the goals of this department?

- How do you see this department (and company) changing over the next 5 years?

- Are employees evaluated on a regular (quarterly or annual) basis? What criteria are used for the evaluation?

- What are the possibilities for advancement in this position?

- What distinguishes your company from competitors? (Note: Impress your interviewer by naming specific competitors.)

- How would you describe the company culture?

- What new products or services does the company plan to add in the next year?

- Would it be okay to call you next week to check in?

MEDIUM

- How long is the average sales cycle?

- Why is this position now vacant?

- What do you like most about working for this company? What keeps you here?

- If you could change one thing about the company, what would it be?

- What kind of person succeeds at this company?

- What is the department head's leadership style?

- Is the company experiencing any difficulties? If so, why?

- What problems might I expect to encounter?

- What is your job turnover rate for sales reps?

- What would my quota be for the first quarter?

WELL DONE

- What is the company's current financial position? At what point, if any, will additional financing be required?

- How many women and minorities are in management positions?

- Has the company experienced any recent product failures or other issues affecting the sales process?

- Is the product development team open and responsive to feature requests and other input from the sales force?

- What is the most common customer complaint?

- Among prospects who ultimately decide not purchase the product or service, what is the most commonly cited reason?

- On average, what percentage of prospects convert to actual sales?

For Your Reference

Sales Lingo

Recommended Reading

Job Boards

Sales Lingo

B2B. Business-to-business dealings such as consumer product sales that involve calling on companies rather than individuals.

B2C. Business-to-consumer dealings such as real estate sales that involve dealing directly with the public.

Bonus. Money earned beyond a base salary that is usually awarded after a set of agreed-on conditions have been met such as hitting an assigned quota, closing an unusually big deal within a specific time frame, or performing at an exemplary level.

C-level calling. Calling on executive-level contacts such as the CEOs and CFOs of a company. This is often considered a requirement for sales reps working large territories with quotas exceeding $1 million in sales.

Closers. Sales professionals who use more aggressive techniques to close deals. These tactics usually work in hard sales industries such as technology.

Cold-calling. The act of initiating contact with a potential customer without any prior contact or introduction.

Commissions. Money earned beyond a base salary in accordance with an agreement between a salesperson and his or her employer. This is a set percentage usually based on the amount of an individual sale.

Customer relationship management (CRM). Computer software used by sales reps to input the latest information on the status of current sales deals that are in the works. Sales managers and executives use them as a way to track sales activity.

Field sales. Those folks in sales who work outside of the office, spending large amounts of time traveling a specific territory selling a company's product or service.

Forecast. A report generated by sales representatives that outlines the status of all current sales cycles. These reports are usually completed on a weekly basis and used by managers to track their field reps' activities.

Hard sales. Sales industries (e.g., the technology field) in which the sales rep has a direct impact on a buyer's decision.

Inside sales. Those individuals in sales who work in an office. Duties involve telemarketing, answering customer service questions, and generating leads for outside field reps. This position may in some cases carry an assigned quota. For those that do, the quotas are generally set on a smaller revenue scale.

Personal digital assistant (PDA). An invaluable tool used by most salespeople to help organize and manage their busy schedule. PDAs are often linked to a company's CRM program, allowing field reps to enter notes while in the field and later digitally transfer them into their company's CRM database.

Pipeline. A report generated by sales reps that predicts selling activity 3 months out at a time. Managers use their sales reps' pipelines to set goals and make sure that all sales activity is on target.

Prospects. Those companies or individuals with customer potential.

Qualifying. The use of market research and contacts to qualify the likeliness of a company becoming a potential customer.

Quota. The monetary amount from closed deals that a sales a rep must meet by the end of an assigned time frame (usually by the end of a fiscal quarter or year). Quotas are used as a tool for individual and department performance evaluation.

RFP (request for proposal)/RFI (request for information). Proposals used by companies as a formal bid to vendors requesting information with the intent of coming up with a package to meet their business challenges. They can range from a couple to as many as 100 pages in length.

Sales cycle. The cycle of a sale from start to end. Includes generating leads, making contact, presenting a product or service, and closing—or losing—the deal.

Sales objectives. The sales goals of an individual sales rep, team, division, or company.

Soft sales. Sales industries (e.g., pharmaceuticals or consumer sales) in which sales reps are involved in indirect selling.

Team sales. Working with a team of sales members to close deals. Sales teams usually consist of field reps, managers, resource people, and legal contacts.

Territory. A region assigned to a sales representative for prospecting. Territories can be assigned geographically or as verticals (by specific industry).

Vertical. A territory assigned by a specific industry. For example, a software sales rep may only call on companies within her territory that are involved in the financial industry such as banking.

Webinar/Webcast. Training seminars that are held over the Internet. Members of a sales department log onto a specific site at the same time and watch a live training session online.

Recommended Reading

Sales & Marketing Management

(www.salesandmarketing.com)
This magazine dedicated to the sales and marketing industry offers a wide range of sales topics from sales strategy and management issues to training trends. The online site offers a career center, resource tools, and a detailed research database for members.

Selling Power

(www.sellingpower.com)
This popular publication targets those working in all areas of sales from field reps to consultants. It offers career help, sales tools, and industry tips along with articles on current issues related to sales.

Wall Street Journal

(www.wsj.com)
Those in sales will tell you that one of the most important factors for achieving success is staying current with the latest happenings in the business world. Insiders point to the *Wall Street Journal* as an excellent resource for those in sales looking to keep up with the hottest trends in their industry.

You Can't Teach a Kid to Ride a Bike at a Seminar: The Sandler Sales Institute's 7-Step System for Successful Selling

David H. Sandler (Bay Head Publishing, 2000)
This book focuses on the emotional and mental side of the selling process as based on the selling techniques of author David H. Sandler. It serves as a guide to understanding and managing the psychological side of the selling process.

Solution Selling: Creating Buyers in Difficult Selling Markets

Michael T. Bosworth (McGraw-Hill, 1994)
This book discusses a major change in sales that is influencing the sales methodology of many companies: the current shift away from the traditional view of the salesperson as a product pusher to the newer conception of the salesperson as consultant.

Inside the Tornado: Marketing Strategies from Silicon Valley's Cutting Edge

Geoffrey A. Moore (HarperBusiness, 1995)
This book focuses on the sales and marketing tactics of the high-tech industry. It provides a guide to the business strategies used by many tech companies hoping to stay alive in today's competitive market.

Job Boards

Career Builder

(www.careerbuilder.com)

A comprehensive job board, with options to search by individual company or even in Spanish. Free for job seekers.

HotJobs

(www.hotjobs.com)

Now part of Yahoo, this job board also has links to a great set of salary wizards and resources.

Monster

(www.monster.com)

One of the best-known job boards, Monster remains a good resource for job seekers. Post your resume, get advice, or scroll through job listings. Free for job seekers.

SalesTrax

(www.salestrax.com)

This job board focuses on careers specifically in sales. The site offers searchable databases, resume help, and a job fair schedule. Free for job seekers.

WETFEET'S INSIDER GUIDE SERIES

Job Search Guides

Getting Your Ideal Internship

Job Hunting A to Z: Landing the Job You Want

Killer Consulting Resumes!

Killer Cover Letters & Resumes!

Killer Investment Banking Resumes!

Negotiating Your Salary & Perks

Networking Works!

Interview Guides

Ace Your Case: Consulting Interviews

Ace Your Case II: 15 More Consulting Cases

Ace Your Case III: Practice Makes Perfect

Ace Your Case IV: The Latest & Greatest

Ace Your Case V: Return to the Case Interview

Ace Your Case VI: Mastering the Case Interview

Ace Your Interview!

Beat the Street: Investment Banking Interviews

Beat the Street II: I-Banking Interview Practice Guide

Career & Industry Guides

Careers in Accounting

Careers in Advertising & Public Relations

Careers in Asset Management & Retail Brokerage

Careers in Biotech & Pharmaceuticals

Careers in Brand Management

Careers in Consumer Products

Careers in Entertainment & Sports

Careers in Health Care

Careers in Human Resources

Careers in Information Technology

Careers in Investment Banking

Careers in Management Consulting

Careers in Marketing & Market Research

Careers in Nonprofits & Government Agencies

Careers in Real Estate

Careers in Retail

Careers in Sales

Careers in Supply Chain Management

Careers in Venture Capital

Industries & Careers for MBAs

Industries & Careers for Undergrads

Million Dollar Careers

Specialized Consulting Careers: Health Care, Human Resources, and Information Technology

Company Guides

25 Top Consulting Firms

25 Top Financial Services Firms

Accenture

Bain & Company

Booz Allen Hamilton

Boston Consulting Group

Credit Suisse First Boston

Deloitte Consulting

Deutsche Bank

The Goldman Sachs Group

J.P. Morgan Chase & Co.

McKinsey & Company

Merrill Lynch & Co.

Morgan Stanley

UBS AG

WetFeet in the City Guides

Job Hunting in New York City

Job Hunting in San Francisco